AF879362

THE T-SHAPED LAWYER

A New Vision for You and Your Work

peter.connor@alternativelylegal.com

www.linkedin.com/in/petercon

Self-published by Peter Connor.

First printing and publication 2023.

ISBN: 978-0-6486002-8-2 for eBook
ISBN: 978-0-6486002-2-0 for paperback

TABLE OF CONTENTS

INTRODUCTION

The highlight of my 25-year career working as a lawyer was receiving the 2003 Sun Microsystems Business Leadership Award. I was one of six people, and the only lawyer, in the company to receive this award from the CEO, Scott McNealy. To have such recognition as a lawyer is rare and extremely satisfying especially because there was a prize of some Sun shares. Sadly, the shares never became worth that much soon after the dotcom crash!

However, there was an even better reward, although I did not immediately appreciate it. Going through a process of being interviewed for the award by members of the company's executive committee, made me think a lot more about what work I was doing and how I was doing it. I was told by these executives that what I was doing was different to what they expected from a lawyer and that it had significant impact for the company. Spoiler alert - this work that I was being recognised for was not legal analysis or contract drafting. In fact, it was not legal work at all!

The more I thought about it, the more I realised that:

- I thought of myself as a businessperson, not just a lawyer.
- Doing different kinds of work – not just 'legal work' – was more fulfilling for me.
- My 'clients'[1] valued this 'other' work more than they valued my legal work.
- Doing this 'other work' did not detract in any way from the quality of my legal work.

- Much of the work that many corporate lawyers do is not that fulfilling for them, and is often, from the perspective of their clients, is not recognised as impactful.
- Having discovered this alternative way of working, more by accident than by design, I realised that there is almost no theory to guide lawyers how they could work to have a greater impact on their client's business nor how they would need to evolve to achieve this outcome.

After my career as a lawyer, I formed AlternativelyLegal and distilled my experiences into a range of theories, programs and frameworks designed to fill this void. Since 2015, I have shared these in workshops with thousands of lawyers working in legal departments and law firms all over the world.

In the course of my work, I discovered that almost all lawyers are interested in becoming better lawyers and they engage in various levels of professional development to enhance their legal knowledge and skills. However, when it comes to real change in ways of working – and by that, I mean, what work they do and how they do it - lawyers tend to fall into one of three broad categories:

1. Those who have no interest whatsoever in changing their ways of working. That may be because they are largely unaware of the changes happening in the legal or business world or because they are simply content with continuing their current way of working.
2. Those who may not be well informed about all the changes that are happening but who know and care enough about these changes to feel that maybe, they should change more

than they are currently doing. Alternatively, they may not be completely content with their current ways of working and are interested to explore how they could change.

3. Those who are aware of many of the changes that are happening, are enthusiastic about changing, and are hungry for guidance on how to change.

This book will be of interest to anyone in the second or third category. It may not be of interest to those in the first category unless they are leaders of firms or legal departments with lawyers who fall into the second or third category.

I should also point out that this book refers specifically to corporate lawyers. By that I mean any lawyer who works for a corporation directly – an in-house lawyer, or one who works for a law firm or other organisation that provides legal services to corporations. The ideas in this book will also be of interest to law students, academics, non-legal professionals working in law firms and legal departments, and other lawyers, such as government lawyers.

The book is intended to provide a perspective on the following questions:

- Why should a corporate lawyer want, or need, to change themselves and their work?
- Is incremental improvement or change sufficient, or is something more required?
- Is it necessary for corporate lawyers to have a new vision?
- What new vision is compelling for corporate lawyers, legal departments, and firms?

- What change to lawyers and their work is necessary to realise this new vision?

Focus on human transformation, not just digital transformation

While everyone else in the corporate legal industry is focused almost exclusively on technology, this book is focused on something else – human transformation. Almost no-one is talking about, yet it is equally, if not more, important than digital transformation.

Most changes made by legal departments and firms do not necessarily result in significant changes **to people** but rather involve changes **to something**, like a system or a process. Digital transformation and process improvement can be important, and these are the primary focus areas of discussion and action on change in the corporate legal industry. These changes have an impact **on people**, but they are not focused on making a change **to people**. Typically, these process and technology changes primarily benefit the legal department or firm and the impact on clients is often minimal.

By contrast, focusing on changing people, their capabilities, and the work they do – **human transformation** – has the potential for significant impact on clients and, at the same time, for lawyers, as we shall explore in more detail later.

Historically, the professional development of lawyers has primarily focused on legal knowledge and skills. Recently, there has been an increasing recognition that lawyers should develop non-legal skills, often referred to as 'soft skills'[2]. However, when this is done, it is usually in a highly random fashion and without a clear vision of how lawyers might use these new skills. As a result, these lawyers may have a few new skills but, in general, they do not use these skills to do different work or to work in fundamentally different ways.

This book and my second book, *The T-Shaped Lawyer Guidebook: A Framework for Your Professional Development*, are intended to address this problem. The first book proposes a new vision for corporate lawyers, legal departments, and firms by zooming in on new work they can do. The first two chapters of this book focus on the `why' and chapters 3-7 focus on the `what'.

The focus of the second book is on the `how' which can only be considered after you are clear on the `why' and the `what'. The second book explains what new skills and other capabilities individual lawyers need to develop, how they can do that through their professional development, and how to use these new capabilities to do this new work.

Reframing the 'name of the game' in the corporate legal industry

The subject matter of both books may primarily be about the professional development and the work of individual lawyers, however, just to be clear, this new vision extends way beyond that. It significantly reframes the main challenges and opportunities for individual lawyers, legal departments, firms, and other key stakeholders in the corporate legal industry, from lower cost and more efficient delivery of legal services to something more compelling. In effect the new vision moves the goalposts that everyone is currently aiming at.

The books literally offer a new game-changing direction for the entire corporate legal industry at a time when 'the game' is changing big time.

For legal departments and firms, a vision is, or at least should be, the foundational basis for strategies, resourcing, work and more. Changing the vision, or direction, changes everything. The books touch on some aspects of the implications of this new vision at a firm or legal department level, however, the primary focus of the books is on the individual.

The books are not about the law itself but about the **practice of law** although, as you will discover, this is not the most accurate expression to use anymore. Surprisingly, there is very little written about how to practice as a lawyer. Typically, you are expected to figure it out along the way, and those who do realise that the secret to success is not the law itself. The books expose this secret and attempt to describe, in some detail, how to work in a different, and more effective way that is fit for contemporary times and for the future. At the same time, the books will help make sense of the ever-increasing complexity and 'noise' in the corporate legal industry.

There are no quick fixes, surveys, case studies or pretty pictures in the books. Instead, the books attempt to translate my experience and thinking into theories written in a practical way and designed to help lawyers readily understand and apply this new vision. The underlying theories and the factual claims are based on the very best kind of empirical evidence: my own experiences as a global corporate lawyer and from the many in-person and remote interactions in my workshops with thousands of lawyers globally, over the last 35 years. That said, most of the key points that I make are supported by independent expert thinking and theories which are referenced in the books.

The original version of this first book – *A New Vision for Corporate Lawyers*[3] – was published earlier this year. However, I decided to revamp it based on some further thinking, with the goal to clarify the new work that is core to the vision. For anyone who may have read the first version, I think you will find this book even more informative and compelling.

The book is not a quick read. It is full of important messages and written in way that progressively builds up to a conclusion of the new vision. As such, it is suggested that you read each chapter in turn and take time to reflect on the key points as you go[4]. If you do want to jump to the conclusion, then go to the end of that chapter which provides a kind of executive summary.

My aim is to guide you in a new direction, down a new path that offers the prospect of enhanced performance, professional fulfilment, and career success. Whether you are a general counsel, a law firm partner or someone who works as a lawyer or another role in a legal department or firm, I hope that this book provides the inspiration and guidance for you to adopt this new vision and to adapt it to your unique situation.

CHAPTER 1

THE CHANGING LANDSCAPE FOR LAWYERS

Central to any consideration of whether, and if so, to what extent, lawyers should reinvent themselves and change their ways of working is the question of `how' the environment in which they work has changed. This chapter provides a snapshot of the dramatically changing landscape in the legal industry and of some key social and business trends relevant to your work.

Wayne Gretzky, the famous ice hockey player, said,

> *"a good player plays where the puck is, a great player plays where the puck is going"*.

If you want to be a great lawyer, not just a good one, it is important to understand and consider not only the actual changes that have happened to-date, but also the changes that are likely to happen. For that reason, even if you have not seen some of these changes yet, you may want to consider whether it is just a question of time before you do see them, and whether you want to wait until then to do something about it.

In the past, you could, arguably, get away with focusing on your work and not closely following these trends and changes. Then, the pace and magnitude of change did not seem as significant and did not call into question your ways of working. But now, the situation is completely different.

So, what are some key changes and trends, and what is so different now that you might need, or want, to contemplate reinventing yourself and fundamentally changing your ways of working?

When looking at the changing landscape, it is instructive to examine the actual and anticipated changes and trends from different perspectives:

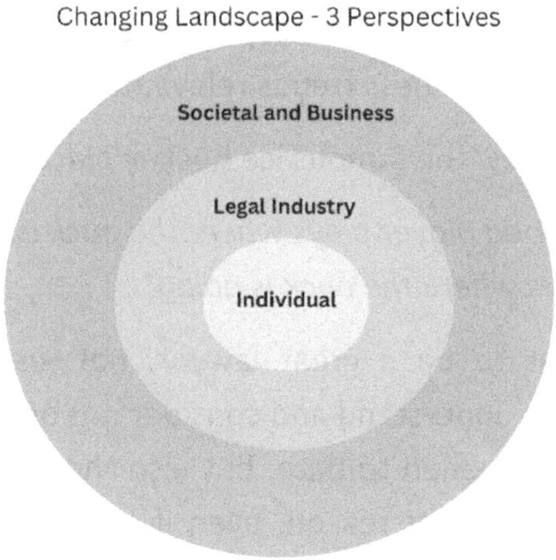

A. <u>Societal and Business Changes</u>

1. The Fourth Industrial Revolution

According to Klaus Schwab, the founder of the World Economic Forum, and many others, we are at the beginning of a revolution that is fundamentally changing the way we live, work, and relate to each other. As he outlines in his book, *The Fourth Industrial Revolution,* this revolution,

> *"... is characterised by various new technologies that are fusing the physical, digital and biological worlds, impacting all disciplines, economies and industries, and*

even challenging ideas about what it means to be human."[5]

Also, as Yuval Hariri highlights in his book, *21 Lessons for the 21st Century*[6], this revolution is playing out at a much more rapid pace than prior revolutions, and that means individuals do not have the same luxury of time to adapt and reinvent themselves.

The time to consider adaptation and reinvention is now for lawyers as it is for other professionals and this book outlines what that could look like.

2. VUCA and adaptive challenges

The Covid 19 pandemic, and the disruption it caused globally, and the rapid emergence of Generative Artificial Intelligence are stark reminders that we increasingly live in a world that is volatile, uncertain, complex, and ambiguous (a so called VUCA world).

> *"In a VUCA world ... organisations naturally expect more of themselves and the people who work for them."* [7]

Also,

> *"... the distinctive quality of business challenges in a VUCA world is that they are as often adaptive as they are technical."*[8]

Technical challenges can be solved by experts with solutions that are already known.

By contrast, there are no known solutions for **adaptive challenges, and they typically require people to go beyond their**

current skills and mindsets, and to change their beliefs, habits, and priorities.

> *"Technical challenges can be met by improvements to existing mindsets and organisational designs. Adaptive challenges can only be met by people and organisations exceeding themselves."*[9]

Figuring out how individuals and organisations can become 'more' than they currently are, and achieve 'more' than they currently do, will become increasingly important. That is precisely what this, and my second book, attempts to do for corporate lawyers, legal departments, and law firms.

3. Digital Transformation

As Marc Andreessen highlighted in his infamous article '*Why Software is Eating the World*'[10], technology has evolved from being no part of most businesses, to something that is used to run the business, and now, increasingly, will be `the business'.

In other words, the focus is shifting from **digitisation** (converting data records from analogue to digital); to **digitalisation** *(*using digitized data, and a range of technologies, to streamline an existing business or process); and now to **digital transformation** (using technologies and data to fundamentally change the ways business gets done and creating completely new ways of doing business).

If your organisation has not already initiated a digital transformation strategy, it almost certainly will soon.

Progressive firms and in-house legal departments are starting to think about this trend, not only in terms of how they need to change to support the changing business, but also to consider how technology can be leveraged to assist in transforming, not just automating or augmenting, the work done by the lawyers and others on the team.

4. The impact of emerging technologies on your work

It is no secret that technologies like artificial intelligence[11] and robotic process automation, are already starting to assume tasks previously done by humans and, in some cases, render entire jobs redundant. For now, at least, the impact of technology on your work as a lawyer has been largely confined to assisting you to continue to do tasks in a more efficient way (referred to as `augmenting' your work) and relieving you from doing a few menial tasks altogether.

So far, this task encroachment from the advance of technology has not placed your job as a lawyer at immediate risk. But does that mean that your job will not be at risk at some point in the future?

Many of you tell me that you feel safe, because machines can never be like humans and that much of your work as a lawyer requires human qualities like judgment and empathy. Machines can – because of augmented reality and other technologies – already display emotions and make judgments sometimes better than a human[12].

As Richard and Daniel Susskind assert in their book, *The Future of the Professions*[13] increasingly capable machines are assuming an ever-increasing range of work previously done by professionals, including lawyers, but not necessarily operating in the same way as humans.

They point out that it is a mistake to think in terms of tasks and ask how (if at all) a machine could do those tasks better. Rather, they contend that **the right question to ask is how the outcomes desired by your clients – that you currently deliver through your work – can be provided in different and better ways**. The general answer, they would say, is that those outcomes will be provided by increasingly capable machines.

On this view, the role of many professionals will not be to provide all the outcomes, but instead, to work in conjunction with these machines by, for example, helping to design, update and run them[14]. The work done by professionals of the future will, therefore, be very different to the work that you do today.

5. The Reskilling Revolution

As part of their *Future of Work* project, the World Economic Forum has identified the need for a global reskilling revolution to equip workers for the future. In their report on the reskilling revolution, they identified two kinds of skills development that are just as relevant to lawyers as to other workers:

Upskilling	Reskilling
Learning new competencies due to change in skills required or for career progression in role	Learning new sets of competencies to transition to completely new roles

The new vision proposed in this book implies a new role for corporate lawyers, especially those working in-house. As such reskilling becomes critical as will be explained in the second book.

6. The shift from working in silos to working more in teams

Recently, many companies have begun to change their organisational structures from siloed functional structures to a more flexible one that makes greater use of cross-functional teams to collaborate on projects.

Examples: Spotify, Netflix and Atlassian

This trend is now extending to many more established businesses especially because of the increasing adoption of Agile At Scale[15]. Indeed, I have helped the legal departments of such companies to figure out what changes its lawyers can make to adopt and leverage these so- called *New Ways of Working* (NWOW).

This development can present a challenge for many lawyers who may not be familiar with working on a regular basis in cross-functional project teams. The new vision proposed in this book specifically prepares lawyers to do just that.

7. New flexible work arrangements

In an increasing number of organisations globally, it is now possible to work part time, less than five days a week, or to work from time-to-time as a freelance consultant in the so-called `gig economy' for a talent on demand business. Even as a full-time employee, you may be offered more flexibility in terms of the hours you need to work, and where you need to work from. This trend has, of course, accelerated, because of the fallout from the Covid pandemic. Now, almost every firm and legal department is required to adapt their ways of working to this new environment if they have not already done so. Lawyers who do work remotely also need to find new ways to continue to build crucial relationships and to learn from others.

8. Living longer and no more 'jobs for life'

According to research in the *Human Mortality Database* referred to in the book *The 100-Year Life: Living and Working in an Age of Longevity*[16], if you were born in the developed world in the 1990s, you have a 50% chance of living to the age of 100, and that age increases significantly for every decade thereafter. The book also reminds us that 'jobs for life', which was an available social contract in some countries not so long ago, no longer applies.

The central thesis of the book is that we are moving away from the traditional 3-stage (education / work / retire) life cycle into a multi-phase life where:

- retirement is delayed significantly,
- you can have multiple different careers and life experiences, and
- you will constantly be learning and re-inventing yourself.

This point is further reinforced by this quote from another book, *The Adaptation Advantage*[17],

> *"... a single dose of education – a process that infers an end state of being educated – isn't sufficient. Instead, we need to swap education for learning, a continuous state of discovery and reinvention".*

In this multi-phase life, it is said, in *The 100 Year Life*, that three intangible assets will be key:

- *productive assets* such as skills and experience;
- *vitality assets* such as physical and mental health; and

- *transformational assets* such as understanding yourself, having dynamic and diverse networks, and the ability to initiate change yourself by trying it out.

The ideas discussed in this book and my second book can help you build these productive and transformational assets so that you can reinvent yourself.

9. The Rise of New Incomes

> *"Alongside the seismic shifts of the VUCA world are equally significant shifts in what people are looking for when they go to work each day. Gone are the days when payoffs to Economic Man alone were enough. In those days, conventional incomes – such as paychecks, health benefits and limits to hours in a workweek – sufficed. Now we're seeing the pursuit of new incomes: personal satisfaction, meaningfulness, and happiness. These are the payoffs to the Psychological Person, to the intangible self, to fulfilment in the interior world."*

> *"But what is happiness? The definition most in vogue, fuelled by the positive psychology movement, is one of happiness as state characterized by pleasure; a banishing of pain, suffering or boredom; a sense of engagement and meaning through the experience of positive emotions and resilience. This is the dominant version of new incomes sought in the most widely celebrated 'great places to work'. Think of flexible work hours, pool tables, dining areas run by chefs serving fabulous and nutritious food at all hours, frequent talks by visiting thought leaders, space for naps and*

> *unlimited vacation time. However, the research literature on happiness suggests another definition, one that is overlapping but significantly different. The second definition sees happiness as human* ***flourishing – becoming more of the person one was meant to be****."*[18]

If you accept the views above, then all organisations must provide these new incomes through not only focusing on the wellbeing of their staff, but also their professional development, more than they may have done in the past. My second book will explain in detail how to do that.

10. The Future of Work

In the last few years, there has been widespread international focus on this topic at all levels – governments, corporations, and international organisations like the OECD[19], the European Commission[20] and the World Economic Forum[21]. Why?

> *"Because if we continue to ignore the clear signs that the future of work is fundamentally different from the past, we will find ourselves wallowing in unemployment, underemployment and dispirited workers and workplaces. To avoid that fate,* ***we must find a new path****."*[22]

There is almost universal acceptance that because of technology and other forces, work is changing, and will continue to change, for everyone, and that the changes are happening now, not at some point in the future. In short, what you do at work now will almost certainly not be what you do at work in the future.

As PwC stated in its *Workforce of the Future Report*[23],

> *"The secret for a bright future seems to me to lie in flexibility and in the ability to reinvent yourself. If you are a great accountant who has prospered by building strong client relationships, think how you can apply that capability, without necessarily having to be an accountant.* ***Think about yourself as a bundle of skills and capabilities, not a defined role or profession****."*

Obviously, this applies just as much to lawyers as it does to accountants.

This book explains how you can reinvent yourself and move beyond just thinking of yourself as a lawyer. It provides you with a 'new path' – one that focuses on what new work you should do starting now, not in the future.

B. <u>The Corporate Legal Industry</u>

Compared to the profound changes underway in the business world, the changes in the legal industry have been more modest, but not insignificant.

When I started AlternativelyLegal in 2015, there were only a few people talking about, let alone actioning, innovation, transformation, and new ways of working. Now:

- there is a global focus on innovation, technology, change and transformation at virtually every legal conference and in every legal publication.
- there is ongoing global dialogue on these topics between an ever-growing number of legal thought leaders on leading social media platforms.

- these topics are top-of-mind for virtually every general counsel and most legal service providers.
- there is widespread and growing acknowledgement around the world about the critical importance for all lawyers to develop non-legal skills.

This is a very significant change in the legal industry.

Example: the *Foundations for Practice: The Whole Lawyer study*[24] in the U.S, based on surveys of over 24,000 lawyers, found that characteristics and competencies were more important than technical legal skills even for new lawyers. As the report states,

> *"We no longer have to wonder what lawyers need. We know what they need, and they need more than we once thought. Intelligence, on its own, is not enough. Technical legal skills are not enough. They require a broader set of characteristics, professional competencies, and legal skills that, when taken together, produce a whole lawyer."*

These findings about the crucial importance of non-legal skills and competencies are further reinforced by separate studies conducted in the US by the founders of the *Delta Model*[25], and in the UK, by the founders of the *O-shaped Lawyer*[26] initiative. Taken together with countless publications and presentations along similar lines, **it is no longer controversial to say that focusing just on your legal knowledge and technical skills might have got you to where you are today but will not get you to where you want to go tomorrow.**

The widening gap between working in-house compared to working in a law firm

There is quite a difference between working as a lawyer in a firm and working in-house. I refer to it as a gap. If, like me, you have worked in both situations, you will know what I mean but, for those who have not, let me summarise the main differences.

General speaking[27], in a law firm you:

- mostly interact each day with other lawyers in the firm's office.
- initiate work when the management of, or an in-house lawyer working for, your client requests you to do so, and you provide legal documentation or legal advice to that person, often in a formal document with appropriate legal references.
- have limited opportunity to get to know the client's business, its business personnel or to business partner with them.
- focus on the quality of your legal advice and staying updated with the law.
- want to generate more work for yourself and your colleagues at the firm.
- will, over time, increasingly focus on running the business of the firm, because it will become *your* business when you become a partner.

Working in-house, typically you:

- interact more frequently with non-legal professionals (your work colleagues).
- Are asked to answer lots of questions from those colleagues and work on larger matters, but you can also proactively initiate work.
- are expected to understand the general business context and to know many of your business colleagues.
- Focus on providing timely, pragmatic, business-oriented, 'good-enough' advice expressed in concise, simple language, usually verbally or in an email, that your colleagues can readily understand and action.
- face ever-increasing work demands and try to find ways to reduce your workload.
- will focus more time on helping the organisation be successful but, you will do so as an employee and not as an owner.

The differences in ways of working – what work you do and how you do it – extend way beyond this brief overview. In fact, the gap between working in-house and in a firm really is significant. This gap arises because of fundamental and inevitable differences in context, incentives, expectations, priorities, challenges, opportunity, constraints, type of work and who you do that work for.

Crucially, if you accept the key premise of this book, then this gap, which has always existed to some extent, may widen further because in-house lawyers have greater scope to do non-legal work than lawyers working in a firm.

Rarely, if at all, is this gap highlighted in presentations, articles, books, and global social media dialogue between legal industry thought leaders. It is important for lawyers, students and academics to acknowledge the gap for many different reasons including the following:

- it might affect your choice of career,
- it should inform your professional development because working in-house is a fundamentally different job to working in a firm, and
- when you read or hear advice about what lawyers should do, you need to carefully consider whether this applies to lawyers generally, or to just one of these two career types.

I have included a reference[28] to an excellent account of the history of corporate lawyers, contrasting the evolving roles, over time, of in-house lawyers compared with those working in firms. It specifically refers to the U.S., however, it is relevant to many other parts of the world. **The key point is that the role of lawyers has already evolved significantly over the last one hundred years and, at various times, lawyers did do much more than just provide legal advice**. Bear this in mind as you consider the new vision proposed later in this book.

I thought long and hard about whether to write a book that covers both in-house and law firm lawyers. In the end, I decided that I could, and should, do that because I believe the new vision proposed in this book does apply to both situations. To the extent that there are differences in how this vision would apply, I shall attempt to highlight that in the book.

Wellness and Well-being

Studies[29] have shown that the level of unhappiness, anxiety, and depression in the corporate legal industry is one of the highest in any profession. One significant and welcome change is the recent increase in awareness of mental and physical health issues in the corporate legal industry. Now, for example, it is much more common for people to speak up about their struggles and there are many more resources[30] available to help those in need.

Being in sound mental and physical health does not of itself result in high performance, success, and fulfilment in your work. However, without it, those goals are typically unattainable.

Wellness and wellbeing are topics beyond the scope of this book which focuses purely on professional performance, success, and fulfilment. That said, fulfilment and doing meaningful work is an important component of wellbeing.

New Lexicon

Before we look at the specific changes, it is important you are aware of, and understand, the completely new lexicon used to describe the actors in the legal world and what they are doing in this rapidly changing landscape. This terminology is frequently used by an ever-increasing number and variety of stakeholders around the world. Many of these stakeholders are not lawyers and they are actively looking to change, if not disrupt, the status quo. This new lexicon is, of itself, indicative of the extent of actual change that is happening.

I will use this new terminology throughout the book and highlight it for your convenience.

For starters, in the corporate and government context, it is common for the *legal profession* to be referred to as the *corporate legal industry* or *legal industry* or *legal market*[31] . In-house legal departments are referred to as the *buy side*. The *supply side* is comprised of law firms and others who provide services and products to legal departments.

It is said that one of the changes in the legal industry is that it has shifted from a seller's market to a buyer's market[32].

Some might find this terminology crude, but it merely reflects an important shift of thinking by some stakeholders about lawyers (and the work they do) moving from an artisanal to a more utilitarian perspective[33].

I will use this legal industry framework to highlight the key changes happening in the corporate legal industry. Most commentary on the industry tends to focus on the supply side – law firms and other legal service providers. I think it is more useful for all lawyers and players in the industry to consider the changes in the industry from the perspective of in-house lawyers and legal departments. That perspective is, surprisingly, not that well-known by many lawyers working in firms. In-house lawyers are, after all, in a practical, if not literal, sense 'the client'[34] and so law firm lawyers need to understand the world from the in-house perspective just as much as in-house lawyers do.

B1. <u>General Trends Within In-House Legal Departments: The Buy Side Dimension</u>

(a) The rise of in-house lawyers

When I moved in-house from private practice at Baker McKenzie to become International Legal Counsel at Sun Microsystems in Silicon Valley, some of my friends and family questioned my move. At that time, in the late 1980s, working in-house was still not that common and had a bit of a 'second class lawyer' stigma attached.

Now, in-house roles are in high demand and in-house lawyers comprise up to one third of the legal profession in quite a few countries. More importantly, the influence of in-house lawyers inside their organisations has grown from what was, in many cases, a mere go-between for the business and law firms, to now becoming a key part of the business team.

The growth of importance of in-house lawyers within the legal profession and the business world more generally can be seen by the rise in membership and profile of in-house legal associations such as *Association of Corporate Counsel*[35] and their various chapters around the world, *European Corporate Lawyers Association*[36], and the various national members of the *In-house Counsel WorldWide*[37] network. If you are not familiar with these associations, I would encourage you to check them out because they have helped me during my career especially in building a network with other in-house lawyers.

(b) The *more for less* challenge

In his book *Tomorrow's Lawyers*[38], Richard Susskind coined the expression 'more for less' to describe the challenge faced by most general counsel – how to cope with constrained internal resources, and in many cases, limited budgets for external counsel, to deal with the ever-increasing flow of legal work arising from organisational growth and changing regulatory environments. Most general counsel I know would say this remains their number one challenge and addressing it has become a huge focus for them and for consultants like me.

There are many ways to reduce the traditional work done by in-house lawyers using what I refer to as *work rationalisation* tools. This ongoing exercise is not only key to in-house lawyers coping with the endless stream of this work, but also critical to finding time for you to do different kinds of more impactful non-legal work, as suggested in this book.

(c) Informal expansion of role (and expectations) of in-house lawyers

Compounding the more for less challenge is the rising expectations of business and functional colleagues, and the desire of in-house lawyers to get more involved in their organisations. Increasingly, some lawyers end up doing work that extends beyond their formal roles as in-house lawyers, and beyond traditional legal services[39]. In general, an expansion of role and work, that happens almost by accident in a few cases, is precisely what this book advocates but on a more widespread, conscious, and deliberate basis in relation to very specific types of work. This trend is not that well documented except for the general counsel role, where there is a lot written[40] about how that role has evolved way beyond the legal area. It should be obvious that if this expanded role and work is expected of general counsels, other in-house lawyers need to start gaining experience long before they wish to move into a general counsel role.

(d) Formally assuming non-legal roles

General counsel and other senior in-house lawyers are increasingly taking on roles, in addition to legal.

Example: they are assuming formal responsibility in a whole range of areas such as risk, compliance, human resources, administration, privacy, sustainability, and innovation. In some cases, in-house lawyers at all levels relinquish their legal responsibilities and move full-time into non-legal roles.

These non-legal roles may not be available, or of interest, to you now, however, that may change as your progress through your career, and it is prudent to start taking steps now to prepare yourself for these roles.

(e) Unbundling of work

Much of the work, especially the more complex, time-consuming work, done by lawyers can be disaggregated into smaller, discrete groups of activities.

Example: litigation typically involves a range of work such as legal research, reviewing communications and documents, interviewing witnesses, and preparing court documents. Not all these activities need to be done by a lawyer, or anyone in the legal department, or in your organisation, or even in your own country. Indeed, not everything has to be done by a human. Perhaps it can be automated.

In recent years, there has been greater focus on more consciously unbundling[41] work done by lawyers. This trend is likely to continue because it facilitates standardisation, automation, outsourcing and right-sourcing.

(f) Standardisation of work

Most lawyers treat each task like it is unique. Sure, you may take advantage of precedents, standard form documents and your own prior experience but, while the circumstances of each case may be unique, often the steps involved to do the tasks are the same. Legal departments are increasingly challenging themselves to look for repeat patterns in their work and, using process design and workflows, trying to standardise as much as possible. This standardisation process is aided by unbundling, and it facilitates outsourcing, right-sourcing, automation or the productisation of services. After this process is completed then the work is said to be *commoditised.*

(g) Productisation of services

In-house lawyers are accustomed to advising and supporting their colleagues on a one-on-one basis. If you can standardise some of this work, then you can turn this service into a product by, for example, using an app, bot, or online tool.

Examples: there are bots that allow your colleagues to obtain answers to frequently asked questions themselves without coming to the legal department; self-help tools for NDAs; and apps that allow employees to obtain gifts and entertainment anti-bribery clearances.

The process of turning services into these products is called the **productisation of services**. It offers the promise of reducing time spent doing repetitive tasks and offers your colleagues speedier access to the information and documents they need.

The productisation of services, whether developed by the in-house team or by an external organisation, is happening in a few progressive teams. However, expect this trend to become more mainstream and widespread in the coming years because it is the primary way lawyers can move away from the current legal service delivery paradigm that I will highlight later.

(h) Right-sourcing of work

Once you start to examine and unbundle the work you do, then one of the things, but by no means the only thing, legal departments now increasingly do, is to decide who should do the work. This optimal allocation of work between internal resources and an increasing range of possible external resources, is referred to as right-sourcing.

(i) Insourcing and outsourcing trends

The allocation of work between internal and external resources seems to go in waves. In the early part of my career as an in-house lawyer, the unstated preference was to do as much work as possible in-house, and to only outsource work to law firms where you simply did not have the expertise or the time to do it, or where it was not core to the business. That would still primarily represent the general approach of many legal departments today, although each legal department is unique in terms of its budget and headcount constraints.

A while ago, some larger legal departments started to take advantage of the rise of Legal Process Outsource (LPO) businesses such as Pangea3 in India. My last role in the Sun Microsystems legal department was to establish a global shared services unit – essentially a captive LPO – to handle high volume / low risk work. Some larger legal departments still do that.

However, in more recent times, that type of work is increasingly being outsourced by more and more legal departments. That has been facilitated by the growth in alternative legal service provider businesses, as explained below. These businesses are often better placed to do that work at a lower, and often fixed, cost because they can invest in and leverage state-of- the-art technology and low-cost resources.

(j) The professionalisation of procurement

If I am honest, the way that I used to engage law firms was very informal and casual. I tended to use my former law firm, Baker McKenzie, because I knew and trusted them. I would scope the work, often by phone, ask for a fee estimate and then check that the invoice largely matched the estimate. I know that legal departments with larger spend were a lot more formal than that, but I also know that many other in-house lawyers, at that time, engaged external advisors as I did.

Now, engagement practices have become more professional. There is widespread use of panels of law firms, competitive tendering, billing guidelines, budget and spend management technology, procurement platforms, alternative fee arrangements, value-based billing and, like it or not, the involvement of the procurement department. Nothing represents this trend more vividly than the emergence of the Buying Legal Council[42] , an extremely helpful not-for-profit formed a few years ago, to assist buyers of legal services and facilitate effective engagements with suppliers.

(k) Technology becoming increasingly important, prevalent, and complex

It was not so long ago that in-house legal departments did not have to give too much thought to technology, other than working with the IT department to ensure that team members were able to use the organisation's general business systems and personal productivity tools. Now, in many countries, senior lawyers and legal operations professionals are literally bombarded daily with unsolicited offers to buy technology or technology advisory services from LegalTech vendors, alternative legal service providers and some law firms.

Now, an increasing number of legal departments are starting to re-purpose existing business software, such as Microsoft Office 365 or Google's G-Suite, develop their own technology, or buy technology such as those mentioned in the section below. Despite this, most legal departments do not have a budget for technology, have not conducted technology needs assessments, do not have a technology road map, and frankly struggle to keep up to date with the sometimes overwhelming, and constantly evolving, array of technology products and vendors.

(I) Data focus

Lawyers tend to focus on words, not numbers. Numbers matter a lot to the business and are critical to operational efficiency. Technology offerings have helped to facilitate this data capture and re-use. In recent times legal departments have been increasing their focus on operational data such as information on expenditure, and on how the legal department spends its time and what it delivers for the business. That data is useful for reporting to the business and to aid decision-making by the legal department.

The other main category of data is knowledge date. Compared to law firms, in-house legal departments have done a relatively poor job of capturing and re-using legal knowledge that is contained in documents and in emails and other communications. Better management of this knowledge data, and providing broader access to colleagues, is becoming a point of focus in many legal departments.

(m) Emergence of Legal Operations

In-house legal departments have always had to run their legal departments in an efficient way. Historically this was done, by either an administrator or by a lawyer, as an additional and often unwelcomed responsibility to their main role, without much guidance or support.

One of the most dramatic trends in the last few years for in-house legal departments has been the emergence of legal operations as a discipline and as a profession. The formation and rapid growth of the *Corporate Legal Operations Consortium* (*CLOC*) symbolises, and to some extent has contributed, to this rise to prominence of legal operations. This trend continues apace with the emergence of many other legal operations communities and organisations[43].

Legal operations professionals are viewed by some as the rock stars of the legal industry and, undoubtedly, they are driving a lot of much-needed change within legal departments, primarily to enhance operational efficiency. Most legal departments of any size have appointed at least one, if not more, people dedicated to legal operations.

So, what does legal operations mean?

In short, it is everything that needs to be done to run an efficient legal department. The CLOC 12 core legal operations competencies as described on their site[44], and as shown below, provide a useful overview of the key areas of legal operations. Also helpful is the *ACC Legal Operations Maturity Model*[45] which provides legal departments with an easy way to ascertain the state of their legal operations maturity.

Lawyers do not necessarily need to become experts in legal operations, although that might offer a potential new career path for some. Every in-house lawyer should appreciate the importance of legal operations and support your legal operations professionals; however, the presence of legal operations professionals does not mean you can abdicate responsibility for, or involvement in, innovation and transformation.

Legal operations professionals can help by freeing up your time and by allowing you to focus on, not just doing your work, but transforming it such as outlined in the new vision proposed in this book.

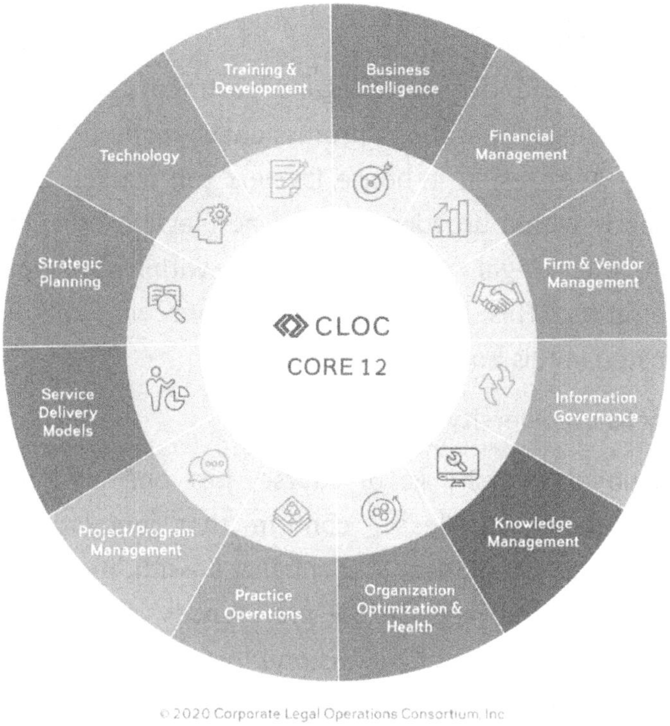

(Source:

https://cloc.org/wp-content/uploads/2018/12/CLOC_CCRM_2018.pdf, Accessed 21 Oct 2023)

(n) Working more with non-legal professionals

In-house lawyers have always worked for a range of non-legal professionals in their organisations, when they provide them with legal advice and support. Also, many legal departments in different countries have, over the years, employed a range of non-legal professionals such as paralegals, contract managers and administrators.

Now, as noted above, more legal departments are starting to hire or engage legal operations professionals, many of whom are not lawyers. As a result, in-house lawyers can expect to work more frequently with a broader range of non-legal professionals either within their legal departments, or within or outside their organisation. This is one of the reasons why the new vision suggested in this book is so important.

(o) Focus on diversity and inclusion.

Professional diversity is, of course, just one kind of diversity. Various recent studies[46] confirm that innovation, and the performance of a team, is enhanced with more diversity of gender, ethnicity, age, sexual preferences, national origin, and physical and mental ability. It is one thing to have a diverse team, and quite another to have an inclusive environment that truly values different ideas and perspectives, provides equal access to opportunities and resources, and encourages all employees to fully contribute to the success of the team.

Diversity and inclusion are becoming key focus areas for progressive legal departments and legal service providers. Nothing represents that more vividly than the Diversity Lab's *Manfield Rules* [47] that are being adopted by more legal departments and law firms.

(p) Enhanced sharing, collaboration, and co-creation.

Historically, for most in-house lawyers, sharing has largely been limited to uploading documents to a shared drive, discussions at legal department meetings, and the distribution of legal department reports. Collaboration has been limited to doing what is necessary to support a colleague in relation to a specific transaction or matter. In recent times there has been a significant expansion of the levels and types of collaboration and the parties involved.

Examples:

- **Within the legal department,** collaboration has been facilitated by the more widespread use of collaboration technologies[48], and sharing has been enhanced by the desire to capture and re-use knowledge data[49], and, in some cases, new agile ways of work involving more transparency into work done[50].
- **Within the same organisation**, legal departments are collaborating more with other colleagues in cross-functional teams as part of new, more agile organisational structures, and are also providing colleagues with access to contracts and information so they can self-help.
- Sharing of best practices **between those working in legal departments in different organisations** has occurred for many years, largely facilitated by in-house associations, however, in recent times, this has significantly increased in the legal operations area.
- Collaboration **between in-house departments and legal service providers** on deals, for example, has been enhanced by using collaborative virtual workspaces typically established by the service provider. Recently, some service providers are **co-creating**[51] solutions for legal departments

often involving **hackathons**[52] and leveraging design thinking methodologies.

(q) Growth of Communities for Corporate Lawyers

The various local law societies and the in-house associations mentioned earlier have long created communities for corporate lawyers. However, in recent times there has been an explosion of communities at many different levels.

At an individual level, there has been a significant increase in the popularity of LinkedIn for networking amongst a small but growing percentage of all lawyers. This has facilitated the emergence of **personal branding**[53] as some seek to establish communities of followers and connections.

At a more macro level, a variety of individuals and stakeholders have created communities typically for in-house lawyers or for general counsel[54]. Many of these communities provide a cheaper alternative way to stay informed and connected with your peers. Most are beneficial but it is important to be aware of the underlying philosophies of the founders because there are potential risks similar to the well-known online communities. Expect to see more of these communities appearing because it is in the interests of the founders to expand and engage you in these communities.

(r) Focus on Innovation and Transformation.

As mentioned earlier, innovation and transformation have changed from barely being of interest to most general counsel, to be an explicit agenda item for most legal departments. That is reflected in the emergence of innovation initiatives, innovation committees and heads of transformation in legal departments. Sadly, there is a lot of misunderstanding about what innovation and transformation mean. As a result, legal departments can point to improvements, but rarely, to human transformation or innovation that matters to clients.

(s) Lack of precision in 'the language of change'.

Words like ***innovation*** and ***transformation*** are part of what has become a new language used by commentators and stakeholders to refer to changes in the corporate legal industry. Other words in this category include ***business partnering, vision, value, 'human' and non-legal skills, trusted advisor, and the T-Shaped Lawyer***. Unfortunately, these expressions are frequently misused and abused and are losing their true meaning.

Being precise in the language of change is crucially important. As I said in a recent article for ACC Docket magazine[55], it is ironic that for a profession that prides itself on being so precise when it comes to the language used in the law – contracts, legislation, opinion letters – how imprecise most lawyers are when it comes to the language of change in the practice of law.

Being precise matters just as much when you are talking about change in the practice of law as it does in the law itself.

If you use these key expressions loosely it will be difficult, if not impossible, to effect meaningful change and to realise your change objectives. It will also be difficult to explain key change concepts to your colleagues, clients and third parties. One of my objectives in the books is to clarify the precise meaning of these key change concepts and to give you a vocabulary to use to discuss change in your firm or legal department.

B2. Changes to What In-House Legal Departments are Buying

(a) Legal advice

In-house legal departments spend most of their external budgets on legal services. To obtain those services, in-house lawyers tend to engage law firms, or other legal service providers, on an as needed and bespoke basis. Although there are some changes emerging about how legal services are procured (see below), typically each engagement involves a discussion on the scope of work, an agreement on the price to be paid (still often an hourly rate based on time spent by the provider) and the work is delivered to you verbally or in written communication.

(b) Productised services

One recent change is the widespread availability of productised services. These services are different to the traditional engagement described above in that :

- the provider proactively anticipates a general need in a certain area such as marketing collateral review, GDPR compliance or dealing with the LIBOR transition,
- the provider then prepares an offering with a fixed scope and fixed price,
- that service is then 'delivered', typically in the same automated, systemised way and, often, direct to the business, not the legal department.

(c) Legal Process Outsourcing / Managed Services

One of the first types of new services that in-house legal departments and law firms started buying about 25 years ago was outsourced services from LPO businesses such as Office Tiger in India. These services were largely for time-consuming, routine activities such as due diligence, research, and back-office administration.

In recent times, the activities outsourced by legal departments has greatly expanded to include contract life cycle management, legal entity management, compliance, legal operations, litigation and investigation support and regulatory response work. The outsourcing might involve the entire function, such as contract management lifecycle, or might be more limited in scope to areas such as contract templates, negotiation, request for proposal (RFP), third-party contract review or contract administration.

The scale of the outsourcing can vary.

Examples:

- The Microsoft legal department outsourced all their vendor contract work to Integreon, that has a large group of people using technology to do the work at a reduced cost to Microsoft. This enables their legal department to work on other more important activities.
- DXC, the former HP/CSC group, outsourced the entire legal department to United Lex.

These days, outsourcing is more typically referred to as managed services, and the number of businesses offering these services has exploded. If there is a difference between the LPO and managed services, it is probably that managed services involves more co-design of the solution focusing on process and technology and more ongoing collaboration, visibility, and oversight.

(d) Talent on demand

The so-called freelance or gig economy has also arrived in the legal industry in many countries. If in-house departments need an additional resource, but cannot, or do not want to hire an employee, they can now retain a consultant to meet short to long term needs. This is an option largely because alternative legal service providers have developed large and diverse pools of legal talent. This talent typically represents lawyers who do not want to work in a full-time role and/or prefer the flexibility of regularly and easily switching from one legal department to another. Increasingly, many law firms and the Big Four are also establishing separate flexible lawyer businesses, and offering these lawyers for hire, in lieu of, or in addition to, secondment of the firm's lawyers to their clients.

(e) Technology

Those legal departments that have the budget for technology are using it primarily for e-signature, workflow, spend management, document automation, contracts management and entity management software. More progressive legal departments are also experimenting with a range of emerging technologies such as specific apps and chatbots, many of which can be configured by the in-house department using no-code software development platforms[56].

Most software purchased by legal departments are referred to as 'point products', designed and used to meet one specific need. In-house legal departments still do not have, and may never have, one dominant platform product in the same way that Finance has SAP, Sales has Salesforce or HR has Workday. However, there are more general purpose, enterprise legal management (ELM) products available from some of the established larger businesses[57], and some newer offerings developed specifically for in-house legal departments[58].

At the time of writing this book, many legal departments are starting to experiment with using generative artificial intelligence to help the lawyers in their work. Not many are exploring how this technology can help clients directly obtain the outcomes they need but I see this as the most exciting and promising application as and when the quality can be assured to a sufficient standard.

(f) Consulting services

As you can see from the above, legal departments are increasingly focusing not just on legal problems but on other types of problems, such as technology, innovation, design, process re-engineering, transformation, and change management.

In-house departments are increasingly coming to the realisation that solving these problems can really 'move the needle' for the legal department, and that they may not have the necessary expertise within their organisations and may not wish to invest in building internal capacity. As a result, there is an increasing number of businesses, with varying degrees of expertise, who are offering to consult to legal departments.

(g) Training and development

Within your organisations, there may be development opportunities and a range of training courses offered, often at little to no cost. Law firms also offer 'free' training to clients and others. These can be useful especially if there is nothing else available to you. However, legal departments are increasingly willing to pay for certain training. This customised training is best delivered[59] through a blended approach of in-person sessions, when travel is possible, online modules, on-the-job opportunities, and mentoring programs.

Unfortunately, training and development does not always happen as planned for a variety of reasons:

- you are too busy and do not avail yourself of a range of opportunities to learn and develop,
- training budgets are cut, or
- there is not enough awareness of the different training and development that is available.

Every general counsel will tell you that the most precious asset of any legal department is you, the individuals who make up the legal department. As such it makes sense for legal departments to be investing in maintaining and enhancing your knowledge and skills through training and development. It is also obviously in your interests to enhance your own capabilities. Training and development are especially crucial to the leaders of legal departments, and to individual lawyers, if you wish to adopt the new vision outlined in this book. Expect training and development to play an increasingly important role over time. My second book covers this topic in detail.

B3. Changes to Who In-House Legal Departments Are Buying From: The Supply Side Dimension

(a) Law Firms

For many years, and for most companies, large corporate law firms were the only businesses engaged by legal departments. George Beaton[60] coined the expression *BigLaw* to describe the business model of these firms. He, and many others, have publicly and privately challenged the long-term viability of BigLaw, and the billable hour as a way of charging clients, and have encouraged these firms to change. Most have resisted these calls to remake their business model, primarily because their profitability has continued unabated. However, some firms have made some significant changes.

Examples: Some firms are agreeing to more fixed price engagements, establishing flexible lawyer businesses[61] , offering technology products[62] and services other than legal advice to their clients including forming innovation hubs[63], investing in non-law firm businesses[64].

There are, of course, many more changes happening in law firms that are the subject of significant commentary by others in the corporate legal industry.

(b) New Law, Alternative Legal Service Providers,Law Companies

One of the catalysts for this push for BigLaw to change was the emergence, several years ago, of new players in the legal market such as Axiom, Riverview Law, and Lawyers on Demand.

Since then, there has been an explosion in the number and types of these non-law firm players operating in most parts of the world[65]. Typically, these businesses initially start in one space, such as talent on demand[66], managed services[67], technology[68] consulting or even talent recruitment[69] and then expand into other NewLaw businesses.

Their structure and operations are unlike law firms. They are not licensed to, and do not, offer legal advice. What they provide is one or more of the other types of offerings referred to above, in the section about what in-house legal departments buy. The largest global players include Axiom, Elevate, United Lex and Integreon. There are other smaller players, many of which are being acquired by the larger players in an ongoing consolidation of this part of the legal market[70].

The expression 'NewLaw' was coined[71] to collectively refer to these new players but they are also referred to as *Alternative Legal Service Providers (ALSP)* and *Law Companies*. These expressions can be misleading because most are not new, anymore. They are also not alternative to law firms, because they do not offer legal advice. In that sense, they are also not legal service providers, but rather providers of business products and services to legal departments and to law firms. I believe a more accurate description is *Legal Business Solutions* and that is how I will refer to this type of business throughout the book.

The total spend by legal departments and firms on these businesses was estimated to be approximately $20.6 billion globally in 2023[72], although these businesses do not operate at all in some countries. As a percentage of total spend by legal departments globally, the spend on ALSP is still relatively small – estimated to be just under 10%.

There is some debate about whether that share will grow significantly. If it does not, then that may well be because law firms and the Big Four continue to build out their legal business solutions businesses.

(c) The Big Four

The four large global accounting firms – KPMG, PwC, EY, and Deloitte – continue to ramp up their legal services business in many countries. They are often grouped with the ALSPs although in fact they are unique.

They are like law firms in the sense that their lawyers do provide legal advice, although typically not in a full range of legal areas. They are all building out their legal business solutions offerings, something I am intimately familiar with, because of my engagement by KPMG in Australia to help them do precisely that. What makes them unique from law firms and other ALSPs, apart from their size, global reach, and willingness to make large investments for the long term, is their ability to provide corporations, not just the legal department, with broad services and products that integrate legal offerings with those from other parts of their multi-disciplinary practice. Expect to see the Big Four continue to expand their geographic coverage and product and service offerings.

(d) LegalTech

For many years, businesses such as MitraTech, Thomson Reuters, LexisNexis and Wolters Kluwer have been supplying software to law firms all over the world for applications such as practice management, billing, document storage, accounting, and e-discovery. In the last 15 years, there has been an explosion of new businesses, supplying these and other technology products and services to law firms and other customers.

'LegalTech' is an expression coined to describe this vast range of businesses although, often, it is used to just refer to the two thousand or so start-ups in this space[73].

Examples: products include e-signature, data and contracts analytics and many artificial intelligence-based products.

Most LegalTech businesses primarily sell to law firms and other legal service providers, but some are starting to use technology to disrupt the legal market and offer new, more affordable services to customers directly[74].

LegalTech is also starting to have some success selling to in-house legal departments.

Examples: the most popular of such software for in-house teams includes e-signature, spend management, document automation, contracts management and entity management.

There are also enterprise legal management (ELM) products available from some of the established larger businesses[75], and some more recent products, developed specifically for in-house legal departments[76]. To learn more about this dynamic area, I have included, in the notes, some references to some legal technology books[77], some useful sites[78] , various legal technology associations[79] and reports[80] on the state of legal technology.

B4. <u>Changes to How In-House Legal Departments are Buying</u>

Earlier, I highlighted the increased professionalisation of procurement of legal services to better control and manage this expenditure and to extract more value. There are many dimensions to these changes and below, I highlight a few areas of new or enhanced focus for in-house teams, especially those with significant external spend:

- reduction in number of firms used often in conjunction with use of a panel list of approved firms
- introduction and enforcement of billing guidelines for legal service providers to follow often in conjunction with automated invoice reviews
- competitive tendering together with RFPs for larger legal projects often in conjunction with automated platforms to facilitate this process
- adoption of spend management software to control and manage external legal spend.

Despite all these changes, the billable hour remains the primary basis for law firms to charge for the legal services that they provide to in-house teams. However, there are a range of, what are referred to as, 'alternative fee arrangements' (AFA) such as:

▪ fee caps	▪ fixed fees	▪ volume discounts
▪ blended hourly rates	▪ contingency fees	▪ performance based success fees
▪ portfolio fees	▪ retainers	▪ risk collars

Adoption of these AFAs vary greatly depending on the country and size of the legal budget. Those with less external spend tend to use mainly the hourly rate with some fixed fees. Organisations with larger budgets are, understandably, more inclined to explore some of these AFAs, at least for some of their outsourced work.

C. <u>Individual lawyers</u>

Considering the magnitude and pace of changes happening in society, in business and in the legal industry, have corporate lawyers changed in any significant way?

That query raises the question of what you can change. In a world of constant change that seems overwhelming and largely outside your control, what is within your control?

Generally, there are two things from a professional perspective that you have some control over and that you can change:

1. **Yourself: your professional capabilities, and**
2. **Your work: what you do with your time at work.**

One other crucial aspect of yourself that you have some control over is your physical and mental state. That is the foundational basis for your personal and professional life. If you are struggling with your physical or mental well-being, then that can adversely impact your personal and professional life. Dealing with such issues take priority over focusing on your performance at work. Wellness and wellbeing are topics beyond the scope of this book but fortunately there are an increasing number of resources available to help you here as mentioned earlier.

This book is focused on performance and fulfilment in your work as a corporate lawyer. For that purpose, your work, and your capabilities to do new and different work, are the two things that matter most.

You may say that you cannot change your work, and that you do not have any control over it, because you must do what your client or boss wants you to do. However, you have considerable freedom over *how* you do your work. You also have more control over *what* work you do than you might imagine, especially if you work in-house. I shall explain this in more detail later in this book and in the second book.

By being precise about what you can change as an individual, we can cut through the 'noise' from numerous commentators about what you, as an individual lawyer, should change. It comes down to those two things – your work and your professional development. Have these changed in any significant way?

Obviously, you may need to change somewhat if you change your role or practice area, change your employer, or move from individual contributor to manager.

Also, a significant focus for lawyers, legal departments and firms has been on enhancing efficiency and productivity. Almost every lawyer does their current work more efficiently than they did in the past, by leveraging technology and other means. Additionally progressive legal departments and firms have found ways to stop doing, or do less of, work they once did, either by outsourcing or other means. There is, of course, new work required to effect these changes.

However, other than these specific cases of change:

- are you doing new types of work or working in new ways? ; and
- to what extent have you expanded your knowledge and capabilities beyond the legal area so that you can do new work?

In short, have you re-imagined your work and reinvented yourself to do new work and work in new ways? Have you transformed from a lawyer who does legal work into something else?

If you have not transformed yourself and your work, should you?

We will explore that question in greater depth in the next chapter but, before doing so, there is an intermediate question that you may be thinking about.

What is so different now?

What is so different about the recent changes and likely future changes that might mean that what you have done up until now may not be sufficient anymore?

Most people would say that the pace and magnitude of change is greater now than at any time before in their lifetime. In fact, it has been suggested that,

'the slowest rate of change for the rest of your life is right now'.[81]

But is the nature of these changes also different?

As Charles Handy points out in his book *The Age of Unreason*[82], there are two types of changes that appear from time to time over our history:

- continuous change (also known as incremental change); and
- discontinuous change.

> *"Continuous change is comfortable change. The past is the guide to the future. Discontinuous change is different. Discontinuous change does not follow any pattern from the past. It threatens the status quo and traditional way of doing things. ... Discontinuous*

change refers to external changes that require internal adaptations along a path that is non-linear relative to (the) traditional trajectory".[83]

For most of my working life, the changes happening in the world have been of a continuous nature. Evolutionary not revolutionary; incremental not disruptive. But have we entered a period of discontinuous change?

The technology advances referred to above might suggest discontinuous change, and that is a view held by many[84].

Often it is difficult for us to appreciate the extent of change happening around us unless and until we experience something dramatically different, firsthand. Many lawyers have not experienced that 'aha' moment.

However, the Covid pandemic has given everyone an initial and shocking taste of discontinuous change. Few expected it. Now, few would not expect, or at least plan for, more discontinuous change, whether the primary cause be related to climate, military, health, technology, or something else.

Likewise, the rapid emergence of Chat GPT and other forms of Generative AI has given us all an initiate taste of just how disruptive technology can be, to our work and our lives.

In times of continuous or incremental change, you can do just fine by focusing on improving yourself and just getting better at what you do. No need for radical change of thinking about the world and yourself.

However,

> ***"… discontinuous change requires discontinuous or upside- down thinking'*** [85]***.'If the new way of things is going to be different from the old, not just an improvement on it, then we need to look at everything in a new way".*** [86]

Looking at your work as a lawyer in a new way is precisely what this book attempts to do.

This chapter was intended to give you a high-level snapshot of the key changes in your work landscape as context for you to consider the crucial question:

Is it sufficient to continue to incrementally improve your legal skills and knowledge and do your current work more efficiently, OR might it be desirable, or even necessary, to fundamentally change your way of working and to reinvent yourself?

The next chapter makes the case for such a transformation, not just an improvement.

CHAPTER 2

THE CHANGE IMPERATIVE FOR HUMAN TRANSFORMATION

Despite the dramatically changing landscape, with the resulting risks and opportunities, most lawyers will not see the imperative to fundamentally change their ways of working, let alone to reinvent themselves. This chapter makes the case for fundamental change: a transformation, not just an improvement, of yourself and your work.

Where is 'the puck' going?

Frankly I can understand why you might think that it will be sufficient to just improve your current ways of working. After all, almost without exception, all the talk, focus and action about change in the corporate legal industry is about using technology and processes for **more efficient legal service delivery at lower cost. That is the way that everyone is currently framing the challenge.** But isn't that an 'improvement', as opposed to a transformational, strategic approach?

To use the Gretzky analogy referred to in the last chapter, more **efficient legal service delivery may be where 'the puck' is now, but is that where the puck is going?** I do not think so.

As I have been telling my in-house legal clients for years, they should constantly be looking for ways to ***'get out of the way'*** unless lawyer involvement is essential and provides some unique value. Any legal service of the type that can be 'delivered' more efficiently indicates that maybe lawyers should not be involved at all. The key to that is the productisation of services, as mentioned in the prior chapter, and an example is the so-called 'self-help' tools for the business and functional executives.

Although he would not be aware of this view of mine, Richard Susskind makes the same point in a different but extremely compelling way. He talks about the importance of **outcome-based rather than task-based thinking** and states,

> *"... the disconcerting message for all professionals is that clients don't want us. They want the outcomes that we currently provide. When these outcomes can be reliably delivered in new ways that are demonstrably cheaper, better, quicker, or more convenient than the current offering, (clients) will switch to the alternative (way)."*[87]

In his book *Tomorrow's Lawyers*[88], he goes on to point out that much of the future of work and roles in the legal industry will be to design, build and support the systems and processes that will deliver these outcomes, with obvious implications for the traditional work that lawyers currently do.

With that in mind, how confident are you that 2-5 years from now, you will be doing the same work but just more efficiently? If I were you, I would 'hedge my bets' as explained in this book.

I believe 'the puck' in the corporate legal industry is clearly headed in a direction where clients will increasingly access the legal information and documents they need without consulting with a lawyer. Lawyers should facilitate this transition and fundamentally shift their focus from just trying to deliver legal

services more efficiently to doing other types of work as outlined in this book.

While my comments above sound a lot like why you need to change, unlike many other commentators, I prefer to approach the change imperative from a different perspective – why you may want to change.

Ultimately you will only change if you decide it is in your interests to change.

A common mistake that leaders make is to frame the reasons for change from the perspective of the firm or the legal department, not the individual lawyer. It is for this reason that this chapter, and the book, focuses primarily on the individual lawyer. Articulating and communicating the compelling reasons for individuals to change, and a clear Future State Vision, are two independent but related fundamentals for leaders of any change management process.

A. Reasons for Lawyers to Change Themselves and Their Work

There are many different reasons why lawyers may want, or need, to change their work, and their capacity to do new and different work. It is informative to consider this topic from a variety of perspectives as discussed below.

1. Reasons why individual lawyers might want to change

So why might individual lawyers want, or need, to change their ways of working, and themselves, to work in these new ways?

Most corporate lawyers, most of the time, can find work and are paid quite well. Despite some predictions of the looming demise of the traditional role of lawyers and rising levels of unhappiness and wellness issues, generally things seem to be just fine. What is the problem? What's wrong with lawyers just continuing the way they are? Why the need for fundamental change?

Well, if you scratch the surface, as I have had the chance to do, working with thousands of lawyers worldwide over the last ten years or so, then you hear numerous frustrations or aspirations such as:

- *I am overwhelmed with work. There must be a better way of working that does not just involve working even longer hours or trying do the same things more quickly.*
- *I'm bored / burnt out doing the same old work and I'd like to do something different.*
- *My work is very specialised. I can do a few things very well but nothing beyond that.*
- *I love learning and I'm not learning many new things.*
- *I want to grow professionally, and I don't feel like I am doing that right now.*
- *I hate the fact that I'm brought into a matter at the last minute, often after a problem has arisen, with limited opportunity to influence the outcome.*
- *No matter how hard I work, or how excellent my legal work is, my in-house business clients don't fully value my work or, for that matter, me. I want to be valued and respected more.*

- *I would like to make more of an impact in my firm / legal department / company. I feel like my current work is largely not that important, and as a result, has minimal impact.*
- *It would be terrific if I could find more meaning in my work. Currently, the work I do feels a bit meaningless.*
- *I feel like I have so much more to contribute to the firm / legal department / company, if only I had the opportunity.*
- *I want to maintain and enhance my marketability in an increasingly competitive market.*
- *I am frustrated that I am not being promoted even though my legal skills are first class.*
- *I am concerned that what got me to where I am today may not get me to where I want to go, and where I need to be, in the future.*
- *I'd like to open the possibility, in the future, of other career options beyond the law.*
- *I wonder what the changes happening in the world – in particular in technology – might mean for me / my job and I'd like to future-proof myself as much as possible.*
- *I want to be more adaptable and more resilient, and I feel vulnerable because I only know how to do a few things very well.*
- *I'd like to be able to contribute more to innovation in our firm / legal department / company.*

- *I'm approaching retirement. I'd like to do something different once I leave this job, but I've only ever done the same sort of work and I'm not qualified for anything else.*

There are a few important points to make about the above list of frustrations and aspirations.

First, and perhaps most important, some of these frustrations may contribute to what is widely regarded as an increase in unhappiness and a decrease in well-being and wellness[89]. This book is not targeted specifically at well-being and wellness[90]. Rather, the primary aim is to enhance performance and fulfillment in your work. Hopefully this will also, to some extent, assist in enhancing well-being and wellness.

Second, you may be content with your job but nevertheless, be keen to explore any changes that may address these frustrations or realise these aspirations. If you look closely at the list above, it is obvious that none of those points will be addressed by focusing on improving your legal knowledge or skills – the default approach to professional development. So, if you share any of these frustrations or aspirations, and you want to do something about it, then you do need to do something different – change your ways of working and your approach to professional development.

Last, if leaders of firms and legal departments want lawyers who work for them to change their ways of working, they need to frame the change in terms of how it might address individual concerns and aspirations. That said, there are, of course, separate reasons why the leaders of legal departments and firms might want those lawyers to change what work they do and their capability to do this.

2. Reasons why legal departments might want you to change

The number one challenge for almost every legal department, as mentioned in the prior chapter, is how to cope with constrained internal resources, and in some cases, limited budget for external counsel; to deal with the ever-increasing flow of legal work arising from organisational growth; and changing regulatory environment. There are several ways to address this challenge.

One of the primary solutions, which I refer to as work rationalisation, is for the lawyers in the legal department to stop doing certain types of work and/or to do that work in different, more efficient ways, with the ultimate objective of freeing up time for the lawyers.

This focus, on the **current work** that lawyers in the legal department do, will help to address that top challenge. However, almost every general counsel will say that, separate to this challenge, they have a number one general priority[91] – **how can the legal department add more value to the corporation**.

There are many ways to add more value, but the primary way to address this priority must involve the lawyers doing **new types of work**, and doing existing work in new ways, to have a greater impact. After all, the legal department is nothing more than the sum of the individuals in it, and the work that they do.

Adding more value also happens to be one of the primary reasons for individual lawyers to change their ways of working.

Why?

As I know from personal experience, the more value you add for clients, the more they will value you. Being appreciated by your clients is hugely important to every lawyer I know.

Attracting and retaining top talent is another reason why a legal department may wish to change the ways of working of the lawyers in the team – to do more varied and interesting work – and develop their capabilities to do so.

Once word gets out that a legal department offers this sort of opportunity, it is more likely to attract top talent who are looking for diversity in their work, and a chance to grow more professionally. This will, in turn, provide the legal department with a stronger leadership team and facilitate succession planning.

Finally, legal departments will want to help lawyers change their work and their capabilities to do different work so that the lawyers and the legal department is 'future fit' and can flourish, realise their full potential, and make the greatest impact. That typically leads to greater engagement, happiness, and optimal team performance.

3. Reasons why law firms might want you to change

The perspective of a law firm, and the lawyers who work in it, is somewhat different to in-house legal departments as explained earlier when referring to the gap between the two. Some may suggest that firms have a vested interest in their lawyers continuing to work in the same old ways, however, I know that some of the law firms that I work with, are interested in their lawyers working in new ways on new things.

There are numerous reasons why firms might want their lawyers to do different types of work or work in different ways including the following:

- Even though almost all the top firms believe that they have the very best technical lawyers, the truth is that most clients believe that there is very little difference between these firms based on legal knowledge and skills. Relationships, of course, count for a lot but progressive firms are looking for a point of competitive differentiation or advantage. Developing their lawyers in new ways and developing new ways for those lawyers, and other members of the firm, to help clients, can provide that difference.
- Firms typically aspire to become 'trusted advisors' to their clients – in other words, the 'go to' resource for guidance, and not just on legal matters. Unlike the transactional relationships that are typical between a firm and its clients, a trusted advisor relationship is more entrenched and can lead to a variety of new work and is difficult for competitors to breach. Firms rarely become trusted advisors to clients, especially business clients, just based on legal work. Being more than a lawyer and doing more than legal work is essential to become a trusted advisor, as explained in more detail later.
- If the firm's lawyers are more than just lawyers and can do more than just legal work, this provides new revenue streams for the firm, over and above legal services.
- Attracting, developing, and retaining top talent is a priority for all firms. Most top talent is more likely to work for a firm

that provides an opportunity, and a program, for them to grow to be more than just lawyers, and to do diverse work over and above legal work.

4. Reasons why business clients might want you to change

Most business clients see in-house and law firm lawyers as a cost to the business, 'a necessary evil' in a world of increasing regulations and visibility when things go wrong. Most executives value that lawyers can help solve and prevent legal problems and provide moral and ethical guidance.

However, they would not typically see lawyers as contributing in any significant way to growing the business or helping to prevent and solve business problems. Unless an organisation has lots of legal issues or requirements, they would typically see lawyers' contributions, in general, as marginal when compared with other functions in the business.

Business executives may not explicitly state it, but they would like, if not expect their lawyers to contribute more to the business by:

Examples:

- minimising any unnecessary drag on the business because of legal processes or systems.
- helping solve not just legal problems but business problems.
- anticipating problems and opportunities and helping the business to address these proactively.

Clients, even though they may not explicitly ask for it, would like their lawyers to contribute more to the business – to add more value. If the best way to do this involves lawyers changing their work and their capabilities to do different work, then clients would want this to happen even though they may not think or speak about this with you.

5. Reasons why some regulators might want you to change

When there is some legal scandal at a corporation, in-house lawyers have, in the past, tried to deflect responsibility by arguing that business decisions are made by their business colleagues, and the lawyer's role is just to provide legal advice, nothing more. Regulators are now starting to challenge that perspective.

Example:

Joe Longo the Chairman of Australia's corporate regulator, ASIC, said that lawyers may face legal charges if they fail to intervene, when they should, in business discussions.

He said,

> *"It's not just about the law. A good general counsel will help boards and companies make good decisions about what transactions to enter into, who to do business with and manage reputational risks."*[92]

No doubt, general counsel and other in-house counsel will increasingly be expected, by regulators all over the world, to be more involved in the business and to provide business input and advice, over and above legal advice.

B. <u>Why Adding Value Should Be Your Paramount Objective of Change</u>

The points raised above cover a wide range of different reasons for lawyers to change their ways of working – what they do and how they do it, but is there one paramount objective of this change?

If I asked you to summarise, into one overarching idea, the primary objective of change, you would probably say something like,

> *"... to be a better lawyer and to provide better legal services and deliver these in better, more efficient, ways."*

That is, in fact, what I am told by almost every lawyer, general counsel and law firm partner whom I speak to about this question. It is also what most of the commentary in the corporate legal industry explicitly or implicitly states to be the primary objective of such change.

However, if the only outcome of change is better legal services, delivered in better ways, will that address the wishes of lawyers, legal departments and firms outlined above? Will it meet the expectations of clients? Will it be 'future fit' for where the puck is going? I do not think so.

Better legal services delivered in better ways are worthwhile outcomes. However, there must be some other result of change that will better achieve the reasons for change, and there is.

The paramount objective of change for every corporate lawyer should be for you to become a different lawyer, not just a better lawyer, so that you can do different work and work in different ways, that adds more value for your clients, not just the firm or legal department.

Why should adding value be your paramount change objective?

There are several reasons why adding value is so compelling as a primary change objective including:

- Unlike any other objective, it addresses the fundamental and universal desire of all lawyers, legal departments, and firm to be more valued by their clients. In simple terms, the more value you provide to your clients, the more they value you and your services.
- As such, it can provide a shared objective for individual lawyers, legal departments and firms that allows for shared initiatives to add more value.
- Identifying ways for the legal department to add more value to the company is typically the top general priority of almost every general counsel.
- It is a higher order objective that addresses many of the other lower order objectives such as doing more meaningful work, being more innovative and making more of a difference, especially to your clients' organisations.
- It is a simple yet all-encompassing idea that can inform all your change initiatives and form the underlying basis for a new vision for you and your work as outlined in this book.
- It is one of the most crucial criteria for work rationalisation.
- It is consistent with the definition of innovation that really matters, as explained in the second book.
- It is aligned with the direction of the future of work as explained below.

Value is a nebulous and confusing concept for most people, difficult to define and to measure. I could write an entire book[93] about value for lawyers but, for now, here are a few points to bear in mind:

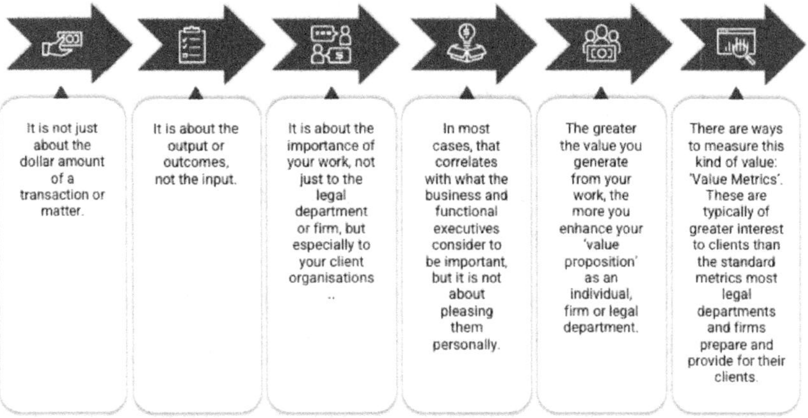

Some recent findings from Deloitte Insights confirm my own view of the crucial importance for everyone to change their work, to add more value.

Redefining Work – to add more value

The articles, *What is work*[94] and *A pragmatic pathway for redefining work*[95], were written by leading organisational change experts at Deloitte. They were referring to corporate employees although the insights apply equally to firms and to all lawyers just as much as any other worker.

Here is a selection of comments that are particularly relevant to this book and to the new vision that I am advocating for lawyers.

- *"Everyone is talking about the future of work. Yet few are asking the most basic, fundamental question about* ***what***

that work should be. *If we fail to do that, all the how / where / who questions will be answered with modest, incremental results because they will be answered according to the work we have today".*

- *"The future of work needs to incorporate opportunities to streamline, to augment and to redefine (work)".*
- But *"redefining work is fundamentally different from automating or augmenting with technologies, or changing the composition of the workforce, or reskilling or leveling up workers to work elsewhere. It is not about adding employee suggestion boxes or innovation / entrepreneur centers to the work".*
- Rather, redefining work is about *"expanding our notion of work and outcomes and not treating it as static or focused on output"*. It requires everyone to make three fundamental shifts:

  (a) *"Shift the objective of work* ***from efficiency and cost savings to broader value creation*** *– not just incremental but exponential value.*

  (b) *Shift the focus of workers* ***from executing routine tasks and processes to identifying and addressing unseen problems and opportunities****.*

  (c) *Shift the requirements of workers* ***from specific skills to enduring human capabilities****, helping workers to learn faster and to better see and address previously unknown opportunities."*

These shifts are depicted in this graphic that emphasises the importance of adding value as the key objective and trying to achieve that by transitioning to more non-routine work and focussing on business problems and opportunities.

FIGURE 1

A new vision of human work oriented around creating new value

Because of more rapidly changing customer expectations and a more complex environment, workers will create value through nonroutine, nonstandardized work. They will use their human capabilities to better read and adapt to context. They will work with technology to see more of the unseen, develop and test novel approaches, and identify opportunities to offload work that does become repetitive or standardized. The complex, evolving challenges will require collaboration in diverse workgroups focused on an outcome rather than independent efforts focused on an output.

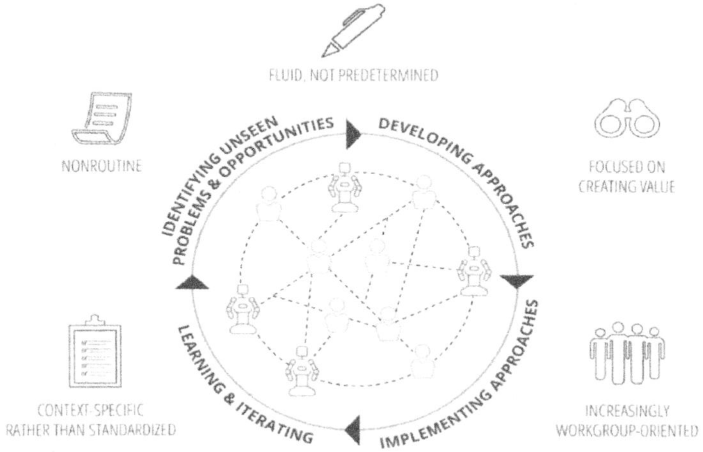

Source: Deloitte analysis.

Deloitte Insights | deloitte.com/insights

(Source: https://www2.deloitte.com/content/dam/insights/us/articles/4779_Redefine-work/DI_Redefine-work.pdf Date accessed: October 27, 2023)

It is worth briefly elaborating on these shifts to highlight some key points.

Efficiency vs Effectiveness

As I mentioned earlier, the change objectives of most legal departments and firms are focused on cost saving and on increased efficiency. Deloitte Insights are not the only ones[96] to point out the problems with making efficiency or productivity the primary focus of your change initiatives. As renowned management consultant, Peter Drucker, famously said,

> *"Efficiency is about doing things right. Effectiveness is about doing the right things.'* He is also quoted as saying *'There is nothing so useless as doing efficiently that which should not be done at all!"*

Here is an overview I use in my workshops to highlight the key differences between efficiency and effectiveness as a change objective for lawyers, legal departments, and firms:

	EFFICIENCY	EFFECTIVENESS
The Judge	You	Your Client
The Focus	Internal	External
The Limits	A few percent	Unlimited
The Objective	Save money & time	**Add Value**

As you can see, shifting the way that you frame your primary change objective from efficiency to effectiveness changes everything. It results in an objective to change your work so that it adds more value, as suggested by the Deloitte Insights experts.

Identifying and addressing unseen problems and opportunities

Let's face it, much of the work that lawyers do, especially working in-house, is about executing routine tasks and processes. The problem with that work is that typically, it adds very little value from the perspective of the senior business and functional executives at the client corporation.

The alternative type of work proposed in the articles mentioned previously by Deloitte, of identifying and addressing unseen problems and opportunities, is something that lawyers, especially those working in-house, are in a unique position to do. This corresponds precisely with part of the new vision for work for lawyers that I propose later.

Developing enduring capabilities

Clearly the traditional approach to professional development, which focuses primarily on developing legal skills and knowledge, will not suffice to achieve the shifts in work that Deloitte are proposing. To achieve this shift, it will be necessary to develop a range of capabilities, and this is the subject of my second book.

Redefining / reimagining your work

As the articles point out, almost all the focus of change in workplaces so far has been on streamlining and augmenting work for efficiency and/or cost savings. There has been little to no focus on '*the imperative to reimagine what work should or could be*'.

This book is an attempt to reimagine, and to redefine, what work of corporate lawyers could and should be doing.

I am often asked by lawyers, *"What is wrong with just improving what I currently do – won't that suffice?"*

This raises the crucial question of the nature and extent of change required to achieve your objectives.

C. Is Improvement Sufficient or Is A Transformation Required?

As explained above, an 'improvement approach' to become a better lawyer is unlikely to address most of the frustrations and aspirations mentioned above, nor will it achieve the objective of adding significantly more value through your work.

Addressing these wishes and achieving this objective requires you to become a different lawyer.

The level and extent of change required to become a different lawyer involves a **transformation for almost all lawyers**. By that I mean, it involves a significant change from one thing – a lawyer who almost exclusively does legal work – into another thing, someone who is more than just a lawyer, and who works in new ways and does more than just legal work. It **is the equivalent of turning from a caterpillar into a butterfly.**

Is transformation for me?

Based on feedback I have heard from lawyers over the years, I can guess that you may have some immediate reactions to this notion of transformation. I ask that you reserve judgment until you have read the more detailed explanations later in the book, but my responses to some common reactions are:

- *"I have spent my entire life becoming the person I am today. I am past the point where I could consider a transformation."*

  My response: This way of thinking is referred to, in psychology, as 'the end of history illusion'. As the renowned American psychologist, Dr Dan Gilbert said in his famous Ted Talk[97],

  > *"Human beings are works in progress who mistakenly believe they are the finished product",*

  and

> *"The person you are right now is as fleeting, and as temporary, as all the people you have ever been."*

You will only change if you want to. But, if you do want to, there is absolutely no reason why you could not become someone completely different to your current professional identity.

- *"I don't think transformation is for me. An incremental '1% 'approach is all that I can realistically achieve."*

  My response: This type of response conflates the aspiration with the implementation. Of course, any transformation plan should be staged in realistic steps over time, but that does not mean that you should aim low.

- *"How can I change what work I do? I can only do what my clients ask me to do."*

  My response: From my own personal experience as a lawyer, I can say that clients will rarely specifically ask you to be more than a lawyer and to do more than legal work. The reason is simple – they do not expect it from a lawyer. However, I can assure you that, in almost all cases, your clients will greatly appreciate the fact that you have gone above and beyond providing just legal advice and doing just legal work.

- *"As much as I want to transform myself and my work in the way that you suggest, I do not think that my boss / legal department / firm would want to transform."*

My response: It is obviously preferable if the legal department or firm adopts a similar approach to transformation, which is precisely why I have developed transformation frameworks for individual lawyers, legal departments and firms that are aligned with each other. However, even if this is not the case, I know from my own personal experience, there is usually nothing stopping you from initiating and driving this transformation yourself. But, even in the unlikely event that your legal department or firm does want to stop you from transforming, are you really going to let that happen?

- *"I do not need to transform because I am already very commercial, understand my client's business and have good relationships with my clients."*

  My response: This may well be true, although often clients do not share that view of their lawyers. In any event, this is a necessary but not sufficient condition for the nature and extent of transformation that I am proposing as I shall explain later.

D. Why Would You Need a New Vision for Yourself and Your Work?

The reason why this improvement or transformation question is crucial is because it directly impacts on whether a new vision is necessary or not.

If you are convinced that being a better lawyer is sufficient to meet your professional objectives, then an improvement approach to change should suffice, and you do not need a new vision. If, however, you accept that just being a better lawyer will not achieve your objectives, and that you are interested to explore the idea of transforming into a lawyer who does more than just legal work, then you do need a new vision as explained in the next chapter.

But, before you sign up for this transformation, you might want to have a better idea of what the butterfly could look like for you. In other words, what it means to be more than a lawyer doing more than just legal work. One of the biggest obstacles to transformation is,

"the ease of remembering compared to the difficulty in imagining."[98]

The rest of the book is intended to help you imagine the suggested transformation by painting a picture of this future state. The next chapter will offer a high-level future state vision and the following chapters will provide even more details to help make the picture clearer for you.

CHAPTER 3

DEFINING A NEW VISION FOR CORPORATE LAWYERS

Before we explore a new vision that might best achieve your paramount change objective of adding more value for your clients, it is worth clarifying what a vision is, and why is it so important.

What is a vision?

A vision is a picture of what you want to be in the future, something you aspire to be. Some like to call it your North Star. Like a bright star, a well-conceived vision provides direction, and acts as a reference point for you on your journey to achieve your change objectives. A vision is different to your mission, and this is a common point of confusion.

Why is a vision important?

For individual lawyers:

Having a clear and compelling vision of the future is crucial if you want to change yourself and your work in a significant way; to transform, not just improve.

Example: if you want to be more than just a lawyer and to change your work to do more than legal work, you need a vision. The reason for this is very simple. Change takes time and you have limited time available over and above your work and family commitments. You want to utilise any time and money you spend on professional development wisely, to best help you achieve your career objectives.

A clear vision or idea of where you are trying to get to, will inform what new capabilities you will need, how you are going to develop these through professional development, and how you can use these in your work.

Conversely, if you do not have a vision that provides clear direction, then your time spent on professional development may not achieve your change objectives and, perhaps more importantly, your clients and your manager will not see any noticeable change, in terms of the impact of your work.

For legal departments and firms:

Most legal departments and firms do not have a vision statement or, if they do, it was written a long time ago and is filed away somewhere and not used in any meaningful way. The reason for this is usually quite simple – most legal departments and firms have not aspired to do anything other than improve what they currently do. If that is the extent of your change objectives, then you do not really need a vision statement because everyone understands the current direction and the idea of being better lawyers.

However, if a legal department or firm aspires to be more than that, especially if it aspires to address the paramount change objective of adding significantly more value for clients, then a new vision is essential.

Why?

- People in the legal department or firm are not going to change who they are and what they do, unless and until leaders of firms and legal departments can explain what the future looks like if they do change. As I explain in my second book, a clear and widely accepted Future State Vision is a core component of any successful change management process.
- The new vision then forms the underlying basis for, and informs, literally everything in the firm or legal department such as mission, roles, strategies, services, and products offered, resourcing, technology deployment, and talent hiring and development[99].
- In the absence of a clear vision statement, members of the firm or legal department will continue heading down what they understand to be their current path, and not necessarily in the same direction as each other.

General considerations:

A company has its own vision, and a common misunderstanding is that a legal department should simply adopt that vision. However, what the legal department does for its business and functional clients is not the same thing that the company does for its customers. So, the two visions cannot be the same, unless they are so high level as to not offer any helpful clear new direction for the legal department. That said, as you will soon discover, the new vision proposed in this book will resonate strongly with your business and functional clients because it is all about them!

An effective vision can be game changing. At an individual level it changes your strategy for professional development and the work you do; at a firm or legal department level, it changes everything including your business model, products and services offered, strategies, resourcing, and even your culture.

For a vision to be effective, it should satisfy the `AID' test. It should be:

- **Aspirational**: it should be forward looking, ambitious and capable of satisfying whatever you believe is necessary not just now but in the future.
- **Inspirational**: it should be exciting and motivating to want to achieve the vision.
- **Directional**: crucially, it should be clear and simple enough to inform everyone which direction you are headed in to achieve your objectives and inform what you need to do to get there.

A. <u>The Default Vision</u>

The 'default' vision – what most corporate lawyers aspire to be – is an excellent lawyer. Some may even aspire to be one of the best lawyers, if not the best, in a certain geographic, industry or practice area. Most legal departments and firms have similar default visions – to provide excellent, top notch or, even 'the best', legal services.

I use the expression `default' because typically, many corporate lawyers, legal departments or firms do not have a stated vision. The above is the implicit vision which they will articulate, if pushed for a vision statement.

Why not the default vision?

What is wrong with just aspiring to be an excellent lawyer or to provide the best legal services?

At first glance there is nothing wrong with that aim, however, on closer reflection, it can, and typically does, lead to a significant problem.

An inward focus

If you define your aspiration only to be a better lawyer, providing excellent legal services or something similar, then it tends to make you focus internally on yourself, your legal department, or your firm. Think about it.

At the centre of that vision is you, your legal department, or your law firm. With that as your implicit or explicit vision:

- Your plans will revolve around asking how can "I" provide better legal services?
- Your initiatives will consist mainly of actions for "you" to provide better legal services.
- Your measures of success will involve looking at yourself and assessing how am "I" better.

What is wrong with that?

The problems with such an internal focus are that:

- the changes that you make in pursuit of the default vision, as a lawyer, legal department, or firm, **tend to primarily benefit you and not your client;** and
- it is difficult, if not impossible, to be truly customer-focused or client-centric. Lawyers, legal departments, and firms speak a lot about the importance of being client-centric but

often fall short of that aim. One of the primary reasons for this may be that their **vision is not client centric**. How can you become more client centric when your vision is all about you, and not about the client?

The distinction between an internal/inward focus and a client/outward focus is a central theme throughout this book and the second book. Changing your vision from the former to the latter changes everything as you shall discover.

How does the default vision measure up against the AID test?

Is it aspirational enough?

Bearing in mind the changing landscape mentioned in chapter one, is being an excellent lawyer going to be good enough for you, and for your clients, not only now but also in the future (or will you and they be looking for something more)?

Does it allow you to satisfy your aspirations and achieve your objective for change?

The default vision does not differentiate you significantly from most other lawyers. Is that sufficient, or do you aspire to have a fundamental point of difference from your peers or competitors?

Is it inspirational?

You may well be someone for whom the aspiration of legal excellence or being the best lawyer is sufficient to excite and motivate you daily. However, will every lawyer be excited about the idea of doing the same things more efficiently?

Is it directional?

To the extent that it is directional, the default vision is, in effect, pointing in the same direction as you are currently headed. In other words, a vision that refers to legal excellence or being the best lawyer (or law firm or legal department) does not really amount to a change of direction. It is continuous with the past.

That means, it will, at best, lead to improvement, not a transformation as explained in the previous chapter.

To put it simply, the default vision may be fine if client-focus is not a priority. It may also be acceptable if, notwithstanding what I have mentioned in chapters one and two, you do not believe it is important to transform to fundamentally change your capabilities, and what you do in your work, to be more than just a lawyer and to do things other than legal work.

I am going to assume that you do not hold that view or, at least, that you are interested to learn more about possible alternatives.

B. Alternative New Visions

There have been multiple attempts to define a new vision for corporate lawyers such as:

▪ The digital lawyer[100]	▪ The strategic lawyer[101]	▪ The whole lawyer[102]
▪ The fluid lawyer[103]	▪ The O-shaped lawyer[104]	▪ The lawyer statesman[105]

All these ideas have much to commend them and are worth learning about, if for no other reason than they all confirm **the widely accepted view that it is essential, for many different reasons, to be more than just a lawyer and to develop non-legal skills**.

Tomorrow's lawyers

Richard Susskind is one of the most well-known and highly regarded futurists in the legal industry. In the latest version of his book, *Tomorrow's Lawyers*[106], he describes a vision of the not-too-distant future in which:

- increasingly capable machines provide clients with an ever-increasing amount of legal assistance, without the need to interact with lawyers.
- resulting in significantly less traditional work for lawyers to do.
- with a few exceptions, discussed below, the new work and the new jobs in the legal industry will predominantly be to design, build and maintain these systems. This work will not necessarily be done by lawyers, nor will these systems and support services necessarily be provided by in-house legal departments or traditional law firms.

While I do not like to make predictions about the future, I do share this perspective to some extent. However, the way I put it to my in-house lawyer clients is that they should:

- as much as possible, 'get out the way' and enable their business and functional executives to obtain the legal information and documents they need without the need to involve a lawyer except to the extent that this is necessary.
- utilise technology, and other means, to achieve this end.
- ensure that corporate executives can get what they need more quickly and, at the same time, free up time of the

lawyers to do other legal and non-legal work, as explained in my proposed new vision later in this chapter.

I also agree with Susskind that the work to enable this future to come to reality – to design, build and support these systems – will not be done primarily by lawyers, except those who wish to move into these new roles. In that sense, the vision he outlines in his book is not so much a vision for tomorrow's lawyers, as the title of his book suggests, but rather a vision for tomorrow's legal industry.

Susskind's vision for the future for lawyers is, frankly, quite gloomy. He suggests a few relatively specific and limited roles for lawyers who are not involved in designing, building, and maintaining these systems.

I believe that there is a different, more optimistic, and exciting vision for all corporate lawyers. What is more, it is available literally tomorrow, not in the future. My vision, outlined below, is that lawyers could move up the value chain and become trusted advisors but of a different kind to that suggested by Susskind.

C. A Business-Focused Vision

What all the above alternative visions lack is a connection with what I have suggested should be the paramount change objective for individual lawyers, legal departments, and firms – **adding more value for the business of the client corporation**.

The crucial key to this new vision pops right out at you when you frame the change objective in this way. It also happens to be something I have discovered from my own personal experience as a lawyer, and in my conversations with thousands of business executives and corporate lawyers.

The key word is **BUSINESS** and the **vision I am proposing is that every corporate lawyer should aspire to be:**

- **a businessperson, not just a lawyer**
- **who provides business input and advice, not just legal advice, and**
- **does business work, not just legal work,**
- **for the benefit of the client's business, not just the legal department or firm.**

This vision also can, and I believe should, be applied at a legal department and firm level as briefly explained in the last chapter.

The importance of business to corporate lawyers is not new and is widely recognised.

If we consider in-house lawyers first, *'as both business and legal advisers'*, first-generation in-house counsel *'were held in high repute and their sage counsel was regularly sought by members of senior management'*.[107]

It is almost universally accepted that every general counsel should become part of the business leadership team and participate as an equal contributing to business discussions and not just providing legal advice[108]. Indeed, many general counsels would largely represent the vision that I am proposing above, however, surprisingly, not even they are vocal about the need for all corporate lawyers to aspire to this same vision and what steps can be taken to head in that direction over time.

It is as if lawyers are magically supposed to have the requisite business experience and capabilities just as they apply for a general counsel position but, up until that point in time, just focus on being a traditional lawyer!

Business expertise and capabilities[109], not legal knowledge and skills, are the essential keys to promotion into senior roles in firms and legal departments and yet, until this book, there has been very little focus on this 'secret sauce'.

For both in-house lawyers and lawyers working in firms, many commentators[110] have highlighted the need to:

- be business minded.
- be 'client-centric'.
- have business acumen and an understanding of 'the business'.
- be 'business partners'.
- provide business-oriented legal advice.

However, the vision that I am proposing goes way beyond these ideas, and it is important that you understand why this is so. These capabilities are all necessary but not sufficient conditions to realise the vision. You could be all those things, but not provide business advice or do business work, for the benefit of the business.

As radical as this vision may sound to some corporate lawyers, to others it will not be, because they already see themselves as more than just lawyers, and they do provide business advice.

However typically when they do provide business advice or do business work, it tends to be done occasionally and quietly 'on the side' often just bundled with legal advice. They do not call it out to their business and functional colleagues nor to their legal colleagues. They also do not spell it out to clearly define this non-legal work and why it is so important.

The primary of objective of writing this book is to call out, and spell out, what business work means so that more lawyers can confidently and proudly do it more often and become better at doing it.

Why is the suggested focus on business so important and necessary?

Ultimately, all corporate lawyers in firms and legal departments work, directly or indirectly, for businesses. Your raison d'etre is to help the business.

Lawyers can lose sight of this simple but crucial fact. That may be because there is so much focus on the roles and professional duties of lawyers as ethical guardians or gatekeepers. This is important but, as I shall explain below, and contrary to what some might have you believe, it is not mutually exclusive with you also trying to be close to the business executives and get involved more in the business.

Obviously, you are more likely to help the business more effectively and, in more ways, when your vision is specifically business focused. Also, **a significant side benefit of focusing more on the business is that it will help enhance the quality of your legal advice and legal work, because of your better**

understanding of the business and relationships with the business.

Another reason why having a business-focused vision is important is because, by definition, it discourages an inward focus. Frankly, most of the focus on change in legal departments and firms is internal and tends to be on things that primarily benefit the legal department and firm and their lawyers. This focus is not at all surprising because of the default vision of aspiring to be better lawyers or the best legal team or firm.

The vision I am proposing, unlike the default vision, is all about the client and not all about you – the lawyer, the legal department or firm. A business-focused vision will automatically result in a customer focus, or being client-centric, because it will force you to concentrate your efforts on how you can help your clients. Frankly, this is game changing for most legal departments, firms, and individual lawyers.

The main reason why the business-focused vision is so important for all corporate lawyers is because it is usually the most effective way for you to add more value for your clients and to achieve the suggested paramount change objective.

Doing traditional work as a lawyer- providing legal advice and doing legal work – provides a certain level of value for your client organisations and their executives.

However, it is important to remember that corporations do not have legal problems, they have business problems.

Sometimes, legal issues will be highly relevant to a transaction or matter, but many times they will either be non-existent or only somewhat relevant. If you only provide legal advice and do legal work, the value of your contributions is limited and, very often, marginal. This simple fact explains why business and functional executives often do not value the work of lawyers as much as lawyers think they should. It also explains why lawyers who only do legal work and provide legal advice, tend to be on the periphery of the corporations that they support.

If you want to be more central or important to your client organisations, it is crucial to expand your scope of work beyond just legal advice and legal work. If you do, not only 'Law' – legal advice and legal work; but also 'Business' – business advice and business work for the business, you will be able to increase the value of your contribution to the business. As a result, you will be more valued by the business and functional executives.

It is a simple equation: **LAW + BUSINESS = 2x VALUE**

Metaphors for the new business-focused vision

If you like a metaphor, the following may help you to understand what I am proposing with this new vision for corporate lawyers, and the shift required to attain this vision:

- *Work in the business not just on the business*

Corporate lawyers work **on business matters** all the time, whether that is a contract, a transaction or dispute, but it is necessary to go beyond that if you want to do more than legal work, and if you aspire to be a businessperson who provides business advice and does business work.

You need to work **in the business** in the sense that you become an equal member of the business team, contribute to business discussions rather than just raising legal issues, and think about the business, as explained later. That does not necessarily mean that you need to be co-located with the business executives, although that will make it easier to feel like you are in the business.

- *Be able to move out of your legal lane (into the business lane)*

There are people in the corporate legal industry who say that you should `stay in your lane' which means stick to being a lawyer and just do legal work. That lane is also a metaphor for the path or direction that most lawyers are travelling along, under the default vision that I mentioned earlier.

The vision that I am proposing involves being able to move out of the narrow legal lane into the broader business lane occupied by your business and functional clients. It does not however mean permanently moving out of the legal lane unless you wish to leave the legal department and move into a full-time business role.

Rather, it means being able to move seamlessly between the two lanes, as and when appropriate. In that sense, this broader laneway is a metaphor for a new path or direction for your work and your professional development as envisaged under the new vision.

- *Wear two hats – your lawyer hat and your businessperson hat*

The expression wearing dual or multiple hats refers to the situation where a lawyer, typically a general counsel, is appointed into another role, as I mentioned in Chapter 1. However, the expression can also be used to refer to situations where any lawyer assumes a role other than being lawyer. I also referred to this trend in chapter one, and typically this happens for a particular project and when it is completed, the lawyer 'takes off the other hat' and returns to being a lawyer.

The new vision I am proposing means that every lawyer, not just general counsels, should always wear two hats. One hat is your lawyer hat, and the other is your businessperson hat. The businessperson hat is a similar idea to the Businessperson Mindset which is explained in Chapter 4.

All these metaphors work best for those working in-house but what about law firm lawyers?

Can this new vision apply to lawyers in firms as well as in-house lawyers?

As a lawyer working in a firm, it is easy to lose sight of the fact that your ultimate objective should be to help the business of your clients. This may be because you are often engaged 'just' to provide legal advice on a specific question, or to do specific legal tasks. Often, for a variety of reasons, you feel that you should not do more than that. The irony is that, even if they do not ask for it, in-house legal and business clients typically do want more than that, or they appreciate you doing more than that.

Of course, lawyers working in a firm should also be looking to help the business of the firm, over and above doing legal work for clients.

This vision can and should apply to lawyers working in firms as explained in the following chapters. That said, because of the gap between in-house and law firm roles referred to in Chapter 1, the way that the vision is applied will be somewhat different.

Does this business-focused vision conflict with your professional or ethical duties as a lawyer?

Some in-house lawyers react to the proposed vision and suggest that it conflicts with their professional duties, and the requirement to be independent, and to act as the organisation's ethical guardian or advisor. This perceived concern is addressed in some detail in Chapter 8. However, for now, suffice it to say that when you understand the details of the business-focused vision that I am proposing, there is nothing that necessarily conflicts with these duties or requirements. On the contrary, if you adopt the vision, it puts you in an even stronger position to do the right thing. The fact that a few lawyers do the wrong thing, has nothing to do with the integrity of the vision, and everything to do with the integrity of the individual.

Exploring this new vision

In this new vision I am proposing for corporate lawyers, the business of the client should be front and centre. As such, it makes sense to consider whether there are any existing ideas in the business world that might help us frame a new vision for lawyers that is focused on the business.

D. <u>The Expert Generalist</u>

The Expert Generalist is a pertinent idea to help us refine and define this new vision for lawyers. Orit Ganeish, the Chairperson of the global management consultancy Bain & Co, coined the expression *expert generalist* which she described[111] as:

> *"... someone who has the ability and curiosity to master and collect expertise in many different disciplines,*

industries, skills, capabilities, countries, and topics, etc. He or she can then, without necessarily even realizing it, but often by design:

1. *Draw on that palette of diverse knowledge to recognize patterns and connect the dots across multiple areas.*

2. *Drill deep to focus and perfect the thinking.*

As technology, globalization, geopolitical challenges, and competition accelerate the disruption of business, people are confronted with challenges, customs, and issues they have never experienced before. I find that experts – someone with deep knowledge limited to just one area – often lack the flexibility needed to adapt to change and can be easily flustered or, worse, be completely derailed."

Ganeish is not the only one to espouse the virtues of becoming an expert-generalist.

> "*We are now well into an era where specialisation gives way to neogeneralism and lifelong learning*". [112]

Others point out, for example, that:

- *"Expert generalists can more quickly adapt to change – they are more resourceful and resilient.*
- *They can make better predictions of the future because they are not as susceptible to the biases and assumptions prevailing in any given field or community, whereas specialists tend to see the world more narrowly and have silo-mentalities.*

- *It's easier for expert-generalists to have breakthrough ideas because they are able to broker or bridge among divergent concepts and insights from multiple fields and broader networks.*
- *They are more well-connected across a more diverse array of networks,* ***adding value*** *to all their connections due to their bridge-building and translation capacity."*[113]

Just to be clear, the expert generalist is not just a generalist and not just a specialist.

The expert generalist has at least one area of deep knowledge and expertise, but over time, develops capabilities, knowledge, and experience in other areas. Typically, this broader development happens through a combination of education and through taking on roles at work – learning 'on the job'.

Why is the Expert Generalist concept of interest to lawyers?

In broad terms, this description of the expert generalist is interesting for corporate lawyers because it still allows you to pursue legal excellence, as explained below, but adds a dimension that can be game-changing for your work. Specifically, corporate lawyers are legal experts, but can also be business generalists.

Most of the general counsel with whom I have worked in my career, and many of the partners, were expert generalists in the sense that they were not only terrific lawyers, but they were also excellent businesspeople. In fact, it is no surprise that many leaders of legal departments and firms are expert generalists, although they may not think of or refer to themselves as such.

Leaders of legal departments, in addition to their legal knowledge, skills and experience, need to have good interpersonal skills and a general level of understanding of, for example, finance, marketing, human resources, sales, product development and distribution. They do not need to be experts in these areas however, they do need to have a general understanding sufficient to be able to run their legal department as a business, and to be able to effectively engage on equal terms with the senior management team, and sometimes the board, as a businessperson, not just as the lawyer.

Partners of firms, in addition to their legal knowledge, skills and experience, must have a general level of understanding of, for example, finance, marketing, business development, leadership and people management. They do not need to be experts in all these areas, and typically, larger firms hire experts to assist them, but they do need to have a general understanding sufficient to run the firm as a profitable business and to be able to engage effectively with clients.

Even if you do not aspire to be the general counsel of a company or a partner of a firm, I can assure you from personal experience that developing and utilising certain non-legal capabilities, more than being an even better technical lawyer, is what allows you to add more value for your clients, make more of an impact in your firm or organisation, and to have a more successful and satisfying career.

Given how crucial these non-legal areas are to success in legal departments and firms, let alone for the ability to better understand and interact with the business clients, it is strange how relatively little focus there is on these areas. It is as if you are expected to figure out, for yourself, which areas are important, and to develop these yourselves. Of course, that is precisely what the lawyers who become excellent leaders do.

The whole point of this book and my Frameworks is to shine a light on this 'secret' for all corporate lawyers and to offer guidance on how to balance your primary expertise and work as a lawyer, with the secondary non-legal capabilities and work that will enhance your career success and satisfaction. The expert generalist idea offers a potentially helpful way for all lawyers to imagine how this crucial balance can be achieved.

The Legal Expert Business Generalist

Just to be clear, because it comes up frequently when some lawyers tell me that this notion is nothing new to them, this idea is not just about lawyers:

- providing pragmatic business-oriented legal advice. This is, of course, something lawyers should be doing, but what I am suggesting goes beyond providing legal services or advice; or
- having better business understanding and relationships with their business clients. This is, of course, highly desirable and part of the story, but it is not, by any means, the whole story.

To be more specific, the idea that I am proposing is that all corporate lawyers should also become businesspeople **and do business work**. Later in the book, I will provide a detailed explanation of what I mean for a lawyer to be a businessperson, and what I mean by business work. But, for now, let me just say that business work covers a vast range of activities from asking questions or providing brief business input, that does not involve any additional time over and above your traditional legal work, to leading a huge cross-functional, multi-party project that might take up a lot of your time and work over many years.

Of the thousands of people that I have worked with as a lawyer, or as a consultant and trainer, less than a handful regularly work in this way. That is not to say that some lawyers are not more than just lawyers, they are. It is also not to say that many lawyers are not doing non-legal work, they are.

Example: Increasingly, general counsels are taking on non-legal roles as explained in Chapter 1. Also, many other in-house lawyers do a range of business work, often without realising it, and sometimes, this is worthwhile and other times, it is not. In law firms, as you rise through the firm, you will usually spend less time doing legal work and more time coaching and managing other lawyers and on growing the business.

The key point is that any such activity is often seen as 'extracurricular' in nature, and done on a random or ad hoc basis, with little to no explicit acknowledgment or focus on this work, let alone on how to be better at doing it. Ironically, in my experience:

- in the case of in-house lawyers, this non-legal work is often valued by their business colleagues more than their legal work, and corporate regulators are increasingly expecting general counsel to focus at least on the business and not just the law.[114]

- what in-house lawyers, and their business clients really value most from lawyers working in a firm, and are often disappointed not to receive, is not just the legal analysis but rather the advice on the business impact and a business recommendation.
- focusing on developing business capabilities and doing business work will help you to provide better legal advice and to do better legal work because your business clients will reach out to you earlier and more often, and it will enhance the practicality of your legal work.

My aim in proposing this new vision is to shine a bright light onto something that does happen sometimes with some lawyers so that all lawyers can do it always when appropriate.

The legal expert dimension of the expert generalist idea should be relatively self-explanatory. However, it is worth making a few key points about this dimension.

The Legal Expert dimension

All corporate lawyers should be legal experts, at least relative to the business clients that they advise. As such, it is important for all corporate lawyers to develop, maintain and extend your legal knowledge and expertise. This is especially important early in your career and, in general, law firms are much better set up than in-house legal departments to provide this training and experience.

However, not all corporate lawyers need to have the same high level of legal expertise, despite what is frequently an unrelenting pressure from peers and superiors to focus on developing legal knowledge and to specialise. From your university studies, and from any work you may have done in a law firm, you have been programmed to think that the deeper you understand the law, indeed specific areas of law, the better off you are.

Specialisation, with deep knowledge and expertise, in certain areas of the law, is desirable for corporate lawyers if you work in a law firm or if you work in-house in a specialist role such as employment, litigation, anti-trust, trademarks or patents.

However, for most in-house lawyers, it is simply not necessary, as most do, to focus so much time on deepening your legal knowledge and skills. The marginal benefits[115] of doing so are outweighed by the benefits you would gain if you spent the same time, or some of that time, broadening your business knowledge, skills, and experience.

Most in-house lawyers do not need to have all the answers to every legal question that might arise in the course of your work. Rather, your aim should be to have a sufficient knowledge of the laws relevant to the work that you do. This means that you want to be able to answer questions that regularly arise; and that you want to be able to spot other issues that may arise occasionally; and know where to go for advice from internal or external specialists in cases where you don't know the answer. In other words, your knowledge and experience may cover more areas of law, and often many more countries, but need not be as deep as a specialist lawyer. This level of legal knowledge requires time for you to keep up to date but much of this can be achieved by updates from law firms or can readily be accessed online. As such, there is still ample time to develop other non-legal knowledge and capabilities.

If you are a lawyer who works in a firm, or are an in-house lawyer in a specialist role, you will spend more time developing your legal expertise and doing specialist legal work. However, that does not mean that you cannot, at the same time, become a business generalist and do some business work, as explained later.

The legal expert dimension should not be difficult for all corporate lawyers to understand and to develop appropriately although Chapter 9 sheds some light on the interesting topic of what constitutes legal work. The business generalist dimension, on the other hand, does require a bit more explanation.

The Business Generalist dimension

In broad terms, a business generalist means that every corporate lawyer can and should aspire to become a businessperson, not just a lawyer, and should do 'business work', not just legal work. As the expression suggests, the aim is not to be an expert in any area of business but rather to develop a broad, but not necessarily deep, levels of business understanding and capability.

The next few chapters will explore the details of being a businessperson and doing business work. However, just to explain the concept at a high level,

1. being a businessperson means thinking of yourself *also* as a businessperson and behaving like one. That primarily involves:
    - thinking about the business of the client corporation, the business of the legal department and, in the case of law firm lawyers, the business of the firm,

- thinking about how you can help the business, over and above the mere provision of legal services or legal advice, and
- initiating action: providing business advice and doing, or being involved in, business work to help the business.

2. business work means any work that you might do for your client, other than legal work. It also includes almost all work that you might do for a legal department or for a firm such as legal operations or business development.

Can a lawyer also be a businessperson?

Even though you may have little or no prior business experience, and the fact that clients or your superiors in your firm or legal department rarely explicitly ask you do this, there is nothing preventing you from taking an interest in the client (and firm/department) business and becoming a businessperson.

You may be your own worst enemy when it comes to being a businessperson. The pride you have in being a lawyer, and the extent to which being a lawyer is part of your identity, can become an obstacle to you also becoming a businessperson. But it is certainly not an insurmountable obstacle, as I explain in the next chapter.

How can the legal expert business generalist idea apply to all corporate lawyers?

As noted in the Chapter 1, the work context for corporate lawyers varies greatly and there is a significant gap between those working in-house and in a firm. How can one idea of the legal expert business generalist work for all lawyers?

The legal expert business generalist idea provides a jacket that can and should be worn by all corporate lawyers, but it is not a straitjacket. It can and should be tailored in different ways to fit different situations. Just as the legal expert dimension varies depending on what type of role you are in and where you work, so too with the business generalist dimension.

Example: a general counsel in a U.S tech company who is on the board and the executive management team can do significantly more, and significantly different types of non-legal work, than a litigation attorney working in a firm who specialises in patent cases. But they both can and should aspire to this legal expert business generalist idea as explained below:

- the general counsel can provide regular business input into the discussion of business matters in management and board meetings and may also be able to take on a business role in addition to the legal role such as leading HR, Compliance, Privacy and Sustainability.
- the patent litigator can, over and above prosecuting patent cases, consider what can be done from a business perspective to improve the client's position in future. The litigator can help the client think through the following questions:
  - Does it have a process (or an effective one) to ensure that the right kind of inventions are being patented in the first place?

- Does it have good processes for storing relevant documentation to facilitate discovery and evidence for future disputes?
- Is its patent portfolio extensive enough to enable cross-license deals with competitors and, if not, what might be done to bolster it?
- If it is being sued regularly for patent infringements, what can be done to minimise these lawsuits?
- Is there potential for regulatory reform that that might impact the business and if so, what can be done ahead of time?
- Are there any general measures that other clients are taking that this client could also take to enhance its position?

The point is that both the general counsel and the law firm patent litigator can, and should, aspire to this legal expert business generalist idea, even if the extent and nature of the business work is quite different.

But what about junior lawyers?

At the beginning of your career, especially if you are working in a law firm, your focus will be on developing your legal knowledge and skills. However, there is absolutely no reason why you cannot, and should not, also start thinking of yourself as a businessperson and look out for opportunities to help the business of your firm or legal department and client. None of this needs to come at the expense of your legal development. It is an advantage for you, and for your firm or legal department, if rather than being required to transform later, you think and work in this way from the outset.

In summary, the Legal Expert Business Generalist can offer a compelling new vision for corporate lawyers, legal departments, and firms. However, are there any other ideas in the business world that can offer a similar and possibly better vision?

It turns out that there is another alternative: The T-Shaped Professional.

E. <u>The T-shaped professional</u>

Most professionals, such as lawyers, engineers, or accountants, are referred to as *'I-shaped'*. They have a deep expertise in one area but little to no skills, knowledge, or experience beyond that specialist domain area.

Example: Typically, lawyers have deep knowledge of, and expertise in, certain areas of the law and their training and development has historically focused on honing that knowledge and expertise. They might add some general leadership, business, or `soft' skills training to the mix, but the primary purpose is to enhance their ability to just do traditional legal work. That is an example of an I-shaped Lawyer.

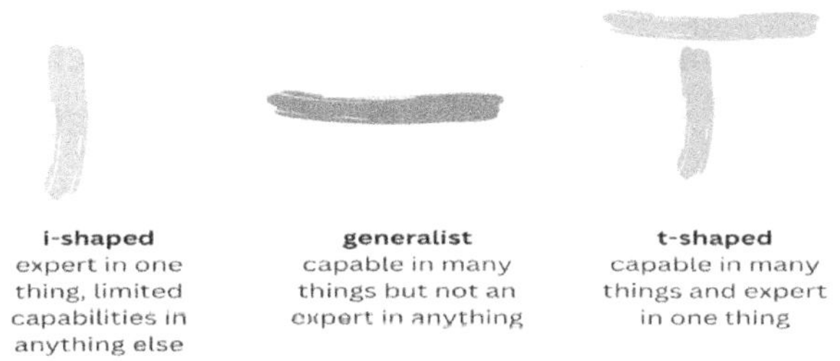

As noted in a recent Cambridge University study[116], I-shaped professionals pose a challenge for organisations that increasingly need people to work collaboratively in cross-functional teams, to innovate and problem-solve for the organisation as a whole. The study highlighted that the main obstacle for service innovation through cross-functional collaboration is a skills or knowledge gap.

To address that issue, their report recommended that organisations should actively develop more *T-shaped professionals* throughout the organisation. Indeed, in recent years, many corporations, including many of my clients, have started to do exactly that. This becomes especially important for the increasing number of organisations that are transforming to an agile way of working, but it remains important even for those that are not.

What is a T-shaped professional?

In simple terms, a T-shaped professional refers to someone who has deep domain expertise in one discipline, together with skills and knowledge from other areas, that enhances that person's ability to collaborate with specialists from different disciplines, to work and innovate for the organisation, not just one department.

If you are a T-shaped professional, you not only develop skills and expertise beyond your core area of expertise, you also use those skills and expertise to do work that is outside your traditional scope of work.

One of the common misconceptions about the T-shaped professional concept is that it is just about developing a few 'extra-curricular' skills. However, when you think about the reason the concept was developed - to facilitate cross-functional collaboration in organisations - it is obvious that developing these skills is **NOT** just for use in your traditional work and **MUST** be to do business work for the organisation as a whole. This is why I have dedicated this book to explaining what this business work means for corporate lawyers.

Another common misconception is that the horizontal dimension of the "T" only covers a few skills and has nothing to do with personal effectiveness 'skills'. That is not true, as can be seen from this often-cited graphic which shows a range of so-called *boundary-crossing competencies.*

The T-shaped Professional

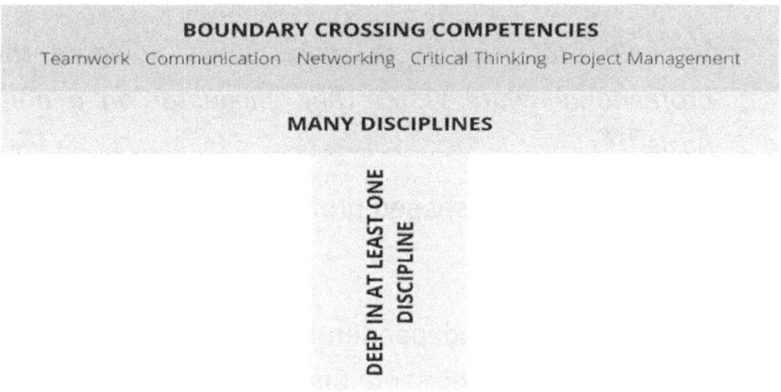

(Source: Adapted from Cotter (2015) and Harris (2009))[117]

References to T-shaped professionals and skills have been around for a while in the business world[118]. Since then, the T-shaped concept has been adopted for use by a wide range of business professionals[119] including accountants, sales, engineers, software developers, marketing, human resource, and information technology professionals. When these professions adopt the T-shaped model, the horizontal dimension is adapted to suit their needs i.e., the horizontal dimension of the T-shaped model is not proscriptive, as some legal commentators have suggested. It can be adapted to suit the unique needs of the profession. This point was reinforced by a leading US academic, Professor Laura Bierema.

Professor Bierema, in an article in *New Directions for Adult and Continuing Education*, advocate the T-Shaped Professional model as a replacement for the failed continuing professional education (CPE) systems in all professions. Based on research findings from other academics that she refers to in her article, she asserts that it promises a more holistic approach to

> *"... help professionals to more fluidly navigate the professional white water they encounter on a daily basis."*[120]

How can we apply the T-shaped professional concept to lawyers?

F. <u>The T-Shaped Lawyer</u>

Amani Smathers and I independently came up with the T-shaped lawyer concept around the same time several years ago. Smathers article on the 21st Century T-shaped Lawyer[121] was first published in the American Bar Association Practice Magazine. The concept was part of my *Everything But The Law* program that I developed in the same year and delivered initially to in-house legal departments. I wrote an article about it in 2015 that was published in 2017 in the Association of Corporate Counsel Docket Magazine[122] and in Legal Business World[123].

Below is a simple, and now outdated, visual that I used many years ago to depict the basic T-Shaped lawyer concept[124] from a skills perspective only.

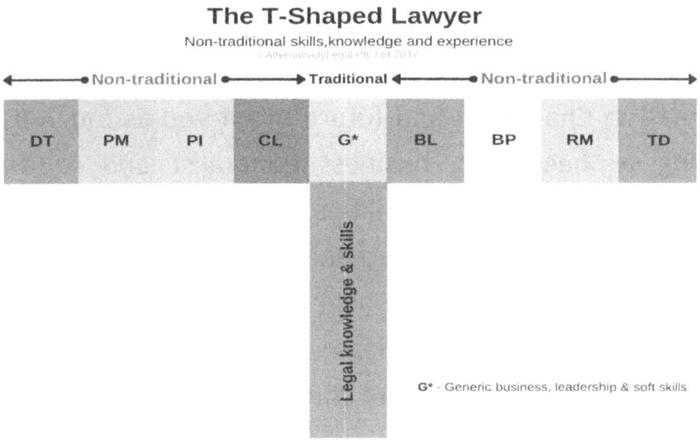

As this graphic of the T-shaped lawyer clearly shows, the vertical axis represents the deep, but relatively narrow focus on legal skills, knowledge, and work experience. By contrast, the horizontal axis represents the recommended development, at a more superficial level, of a wider range of what I referred to as 'non-traditional' capabilities. **The one point that I have always highlighted since 2004[125] is that the primary reason to develop these non-traditional capabilities is to do non-legal work[126].**

This notion of the T-Shaped Lawyer sounds a lot like the Legal Expert Business Generalist, doesn't it? It does because the T-shaped professional is an expert generalist – just a slightly more specific version of one.

Which idea – the T-Shaped Lawyer or the Legal Expert Business Generalist - offers the best vision for corporate lawyers?

T-Shaped Lawyer vs The Legal Expert Business Generalist

Both ideas offer compelling visions for lawyers and either one represents an excellent choice. Both satisfy the AID test. They are aspirational in that they aim to address the key change objectives outlined in Chapter 2, and future-proof you as much as possible. Aiming to become a business generalist and to expand the horizontal non-legal capabilities and experience is inspirational and something to get excited about, if for no other reason than it involves learning and personal growth. Finally, they are both directional in that they indicate, quite clearly, what changes you need to make to yourself and your work.

However, although both represent viable visions, I believe the T-Shaped Lawyer is preferable because:

- while the Legal Expert Business Generalist is literally descriptive of the vision that I am proposing, it is a bit of a mouthful to say. The T-Shaped Lawyer is catchier.
- the T-shape is an easy-to-understand symbol of the underlying idea behind the new vision – depth in law and breadth in business – and, as such, should help to explain the idea to others.
- The T-shaped professional idea is more widely known and used in the business world and, as such, your business clients are more likely to readily understand what you are aspiring to be, and to support this vision.

- when it comes to turning the vision into reality, as I shall explain more in the final chapter and second book, the T-shaped idea works better to represent the framework of different components involved.

I chose to include the reference in this book to the Legal Expert Business Generalist because it is a useful intermediate concept to help you more easily understand the key message from this book about you changing in a fundamental and very specific way so that you can make changes to what work you do, and how you do it, to achieve a very specific objective.

The other reason that I chose to refer to the Legal Expert Business Generalist in this book is to offer an alternative name for the vision for those who buy into the key message of this book but prefer not to refer to the T-Shaped Lawyer. I know that there are some people who have expressed reservations about the T-shaped lawyer concept. Typically, these reservations are based on fundamental misunderstandings.

Dispelling myths about the T-Shaped Lawyer concept

Below are some examples of comments that I have heard about the T-Shaped Lawyer concept together with my response:

- *The T-Shaped Lawyer is an 'old, out-of-date model'*

  My Response: As mentioned earlier, the idea was raised as a broad concept about 9 years ago. However, most lawyers have never heard of the T-shaped professional model, let alone the T-Shaped Lawyer concept. Of the minority that have heard of the concept, very few have taken the time to understand the details of the model or tried adopting it.

This T-Shaped Lawyer vision is quite different from the T-Shaped Lawyer concept as explained by others. It has been refined and developed over the last 9 years together with the T-Shaped Lawyer Framework™ which is unique and very new. Both the vision and the Framework are more relevant now than ever, especially because of the changing landscape for lawyers outlined in Chapter 1.

- *My T-Shaped Lawyer vision is not new because lawyers are business partners and do understand the business and provide business advice*

  My Response: Only a few lawyers that I have met fit this description but, even then, this does not make you a T-Shaped Lawyer. The vision of a T-Shaped Lawyer I outline involves much more than that, as explained in this and the second book.

- *The T-Shaped Lawyer concept involves just a few random non-legal skills*

  My Response: It may be true that when others describe the T-Shaped Lawyer concept, they appear to select random non-legal skills. However, as explained in my second book, skills are only one part of 'how' you can become a T-Shaped Lawyer. You also need competencies, qualities, knowledge, and mindsets, and the ones identified in the Framework are anything but random. They are specifically selected to achieve the objective of becoming a T-Shaped Lawyer as defined in this book. Understanding 'what' a T-Shaped Lawyer is and what work such a lawyer does is essential before you can decide what skills and other capabilities are necessary to achieve the new vision.

- *The T-Shaped Lawyer skills do not include crucial human or personal effectiveness skills*

  My Response: Again, it may be true that when others describe the T-Shaped Lawyer, they select skills that do not extend to human or personal effectiveness skills. However, the T-shaped professional concept extends to such skills which are referred to as boundary-crossing competencies as mentioned above. Also, my T-Shaped Lawyer Framework covers a range of human qualities and behavioural competencies as you will see when you read the second book.

Hopefully reading both books will clear up any misunderstandings and convince you that the T-Shaped Lawyer is a new vision worth considering. But, if not, you can also use the Legal Expert Business Generalist as your vision and the comments in both books apply with equal force. What is important is not so much the name you choose for the vision, but rather the essential idea – expanding the work that you do and your capability to do new work.

To summarise, I am proposing the T-Shaped Lawyer, as shown below, as the new vision for all corporate lawyers and will refer to it as such from this point on both books.

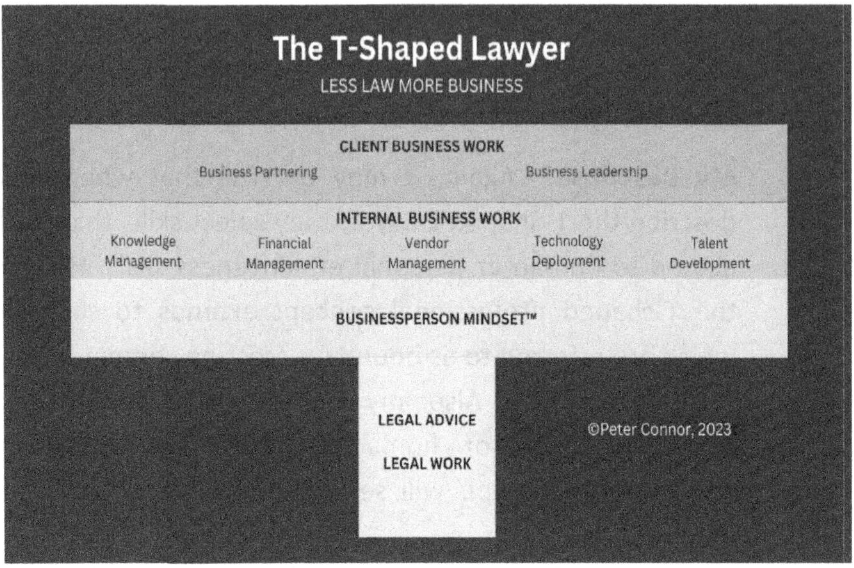

This vision can apply to all corporate lawyers but how it applies will vary depending on a various factors including your role, the stage of your career and your company/ firm as I will explain later.

The next few chapters will provide details on each aspect of this vision, and especially, what it means to become a businessperson, and what it means to do client business work as well as support internal business work.

CHAPTER 4

BEING A BUSINESSPERSON

The first part of the T-Shaped Lawyer vision is for you to become a businessperson in addition to being a lawyer. What does it mean to be a businessperson?

Are you a businessperson if you:

- are business minded?
- have business acumen?
- understand the business?
- develop some business skills?
- are a business partner?

No.

You can be all these things and yet not think of yourself and behave like a businessperson. These things are important, and part of being a businessperson, but there is much more to it than that, and the difference is more than semantic.

Being a businessperson means **thinking** of yourself, and **behaving,** as if you are:

1. in the case of an in-house lawyer:

- part of the leadership team of the legal department; and
- part of the relevant management team for the business or functional executives that you most directly support.

2. in the case of a law firm lawyer:

- part of the partnership of the firm;
- an extended part of the leadership team of the in-house legal departments that you most frequently interact with; and
- an extended part of relevant business or functional management teams that you most frequently interact with.

You may, or may not, have been appointed as a leader, partner, or member of such leadership or management teams. However, being a businessperson means that you think and, over time, behave **as if you are**.

The 'thinking' component of being a businessperson involves your mindset. The 'behaving' component involves what activities you do at work. This chapter will focus on the thinking aspect and the following chapters will focus on the behaving aspect.

The starting point for a corporate lawyer to realise the vision of the T-Shaped Lawyer is to stop thinking of yourself as just a lawyer and to start thinking of yourself also as a businessperson.

The necessity to have what I refer to as a Businessperson Mindset applies especially to lawyers working in-house. It also applies to lawyers working in a firm, but it manifests itself in slightly different ways as I shall explain below.

A. The Businessperson Mindset™

In simple terms, switching from what I refer to as a *Just-A-Lawyer Mindset* to what I have called a **Businessperson Mindset[127] is like taking off one pair of glasses, with a narrow angle that only allows you to see legal issues, and replacing them with another**

pair of glasses, with a wider angle that allows you to see a broader perspective including business issues.

I have developed a detailed tool to help you assess whether you have a Businessperson Mindset because often, people believe that they have a particular mindset, but the results of an objective assessment suggest otherwise. The graphic below provides you with a general idea of the concept of the Businessperson Mindset.

	Just A Lawyer	Businessperson
Perspective of self	Lawyer	Businessperson&Lawyer
Perspective of team	Legal	Legal & Management
Daily focus	Legal tasks	Legal & Business work
Understand business	Just enough	Broad understanding
Curiosity	Just for tasks	Everything of interest
Business trends	Don't follow	Follow regularly
Initiative	Reactive	Proactive
Work involvement	Legal area only	Beyond legal

The Businessperson Mindset™

How does the Businessperson mindset apply to corporate lawyers working in legal departments and in law firms?

In-house lawyers

As an in-house lawyer, you will have a Businessperson Mindset if you think of yourself as part of the management team of the company – not just the legal department – whether you are or not. That management team may be the executive management team of the entire company, or it may be a management team of a business unit, product group or geographic region, if you support that team or your work relates primarily to that team. The point is that you do not think of yourself as just a member of the legal department but, rather, think of yourself also as an owner or leader of the company.

This applies as much to junior lawyers as it does to senior lawyers.

Below are some quotes from prominent former general counsel describing their view of what is required of in-house lawyers:

Examples:

- *"We are not lawyers. We are businesspeople, with legal training forged into a cohesive team committed to the success of FMC"* ~ Jeff Carr, when he was General Counsel of FMC Technologies.
- *"(You) need to be a businessperson first and a lawyer second – not a lawyer that understands the business, but a businessperson that happens to be a lawyer'"* ~ Marla Persky when she was General Counsel of Boehringher Ingelheim.
- The CEO of DXC (the merged CSC and HP Enterprise Division) said he sees DXC lawyers as *"business and tech-knowledgeable resources with legal expertise"*.

Having a Businessperson Mindset means that, while performing your work, you will:

- constantly think about the business of the company, and the business of running the legal department.

- take time to follow macro-economic, social, and political trends and consider their impact on the business.
- keep up to date on the dynamics of your industry.
- be hungry for information about the business, read relevant internal communications and regularly speak to colleagues in a range of functions.
- be curious about the business and ask questions especially if anything does not make sense to you.
- look out for business problems, even before they materialise, and ponder why these problems arise.
- constantly consider ways to solve business problems and to improve the business; and
- get involved even if it is beyond your official area of responsibility.

By contrast, if you have a Just-A-Lawyer mindset, you will:

- think of yourself as a lawyer who works for the legal department.
- focus on doing your traditional daily tasks, spotting legal issues, and advising on legal risk.
- develop an understanding of the business but only to the extent necessary to do your work, and no more.
- not be curious about the business.
- be too busy with your legal work to find the time to develop networks throughout the organisation.
- If there is a problem outside your area of responsibility, you will think that this is someone else's problem to fix it, and you will not get involved.

Law firm lawyers

As a lawyer working in a firm, you will have a Businessperson Mindset if you think of yourself as a partner in the firm whether you are or not and, at least for your primary clients, you will think of yourself as an extended member of their legal and business teams.

Having a Businessperson Mindset means that while doing your work, you will:

- think about the business of the firm and how you might be able to help.
- think about the challenges facing your clients and whether there are ways that the firm might be able to assist.
- be curious about the changes happening in the legal industry and consider what the firm might proactively do to not only survive but thrive in the future.
- understand that your in-house lawyer clients may also be aiming to be T-Shaped Lawyers and that this may result in a wider variety of ways that you, and the firm, might be able to assist them.

By contrast, if you have a Just-A-Lawyer Mindset, you will:

- think of yourself as a legal specialist
- focus your professional development almost exclusively on enhancing your understanding of the law and your legal skills.
- place a premium on the quality of your legal advice and consider it less important to deliver your advice in simple terms that the business clients can easily understand and act upon.

- be too busy doing legal work to worry about the operational challenges and opportunities of the firm or your clients, preferring to leave that to others.
- for a similar reason, also not take much interest in the changes happening in the legal industry or consider what the firm might do to maintain or enhance its competitive position.

Can you change your mindset?

Mindsets are just beliefs in your mind, and you can change your mind.

Neuroscience shows us that our brains continue to develop and change, even as adults. The brain is like plastic, and can be reshaped over time, forming new neural pathways. Neuroscientists call this tendency `neuroplasticity'. These neural pathways are developed by doing or thinking – the things that we do or say more often become hard-wired into our brains as habits. These form defined 'routes' in our brain, which become easier to use over time.

As a prominent social psychologist states, based on extensive research,

> *"... mindsets can be changed, and that significant changes in attitudes and behaviour can occur as a result. In other words, our mindset is discretionary. It's something we have the power to revise if we want to—when we become aware of what our mindset is."*[128]

There are various techniques that can be used to change your mindset, and these are explained in more detail in the second book.

B. Obstacles for Lawyers to Adopt a Businessperson Mindset

There are two primary obstacles that may make it difficult for you to adopt a businessperson mindset; your identity as a lawyer and a feeling that, as a lawyer you are special.

Your identity as a lawyer

One of the biggest obstacles to thinking of yourself as a businessperson is the time, effort, and money you have invested to become a lawyer, and the common misconception that adopting a businessperson mindset would mean throwing that investment away. You have done well to get into law school and even better to graduate. You may have spent years developing your legal knowledge and skills. You are proud to be a lawyer – a member of the exclusive 'club' of legal professionals. Being a lawyer may be a huge part of your identity and may extend beyond your professional life into your personal life.

However, this identity is:

> *"... also an anchor that makes the necessary re-imagining of work much, much harder than it needs to be. It is the barrier to making the crossing from the past of work to the future of work. But cross it we must. The ability to adapt is our key advantage.*
>
> *The first step to seizing that advantage is letting go of our professional identity, and in letting go, tapping into our imaginations to re-imagine ourselves and our work".*[129]

Letting go of your identity as a lawyer is not the same thing as abandoning or quitting your role as a lawyer. Rather, it means to not associate yourself so strongly, or only, with this one idea of being a lawyer. It means not showing your lawyer badge so prominently, especially when interacting with the business and functional executives at the organisation. It means creating enough mental space for you to also think of yourself as something else – a businessperson.

Feeling as if you are special, maybe even superior

A related, but separate, obstacle to adopting a businessperson mindset is feeling that, as a lawyer, you are special and different from the business and functional executives at the client organisation. Feeling this way is understandable, especially if you have worked daily in a law firm together with other equally smart and impressive lawyers. Often, when a lawyer moves from working in a firm to an in-house job, they think that their non-legal colleagues are not as intelligent; and in extreme cases, this can lead to a sense of superiority, disrespect and a 'them and us' mentality.

If you do think of yourself as special or superior, then this mindset will make it difficult to adopt a businessperson mindset. It will be an impediment to engaging effectively with business clients, if you work in a firm, and it will be an impediment to you becoming successful in an in-house role.

When I started my first in-house role at Sun Microsystems in California, I soon realised that no matter what I might have thought about myself and my fellow lawyers, it was the engineers who were considered special, and certainly not the lawyers. I quickly learnt that whatever I might have thought about my non-legal colleagues, in my case a regional sales, service and marketing team, the best way for me to be successful was to become part of that team.

Thinking of yourself as a team player, as you would in a team sport, may be a helpful analogy to adopting the businessperson mindset. Your 'legal smarts' will be appreciated but no more so than the smarts that your fellow colleagues bring to the team. Over time, with a businessperson mindset, you will develop your own level of 'business smarts' and you will soon realise that it is these smarts that are generally valued more than your legal smarts. Once you experience that feeling, it will help you to identify yourself as a businessperson, not just a lawyer.

Finally, the fact that as a lawyer, you have professional obligations that do not apply to other employees means that you have special responsibilities. It does not mean that you must consider yourself as special.

Adopting a Businessperson Mindset is not about giving anything up. It is not about losing anything but, rather, adding something. It is about building on that base of being a lawyer and a part of the legal department or firm. It is about becoming more than just a lawyer. It is about becoming a real or virtual part of the relevant business team in your client organisation.

Having a Businessperson Mindset is a critical enabler to becoming a businessperson. However, being a businessperson involves more than thinking of yourself as a businessperson. It means behaving like one.

The next few chapters will explain what behaving like a businessperson involves, by examining in detail, what types of business work you can, and should, do if you wish to be a T-Shaped Lawyer.

CHAPTER 5

DOING BUSINESS WORK

To be a businessperson, and to become a T-Shaped Lawyer, you should not only think of yourself as a businessperson. You also need to behave like one. That means you must translate that thinking into action. **In simple terms, you need to do business work, not just legal work, for the benefit of the client organisation and not just the legal department or firm**.

Let's unpack this statement by exploring the notion of business work for corporate lawyers. In a very general sense, almost all work[130] that you do in a legal department or law firm other than legal work[131] can be said to be business work. Some of that work you should be doing less of and some of that work you should be doing more of.

To clarify what type of business work you should be doing more of, I have refined my explanation of business work somewhat since the first edition of this book and it is depicted in the graphic below.

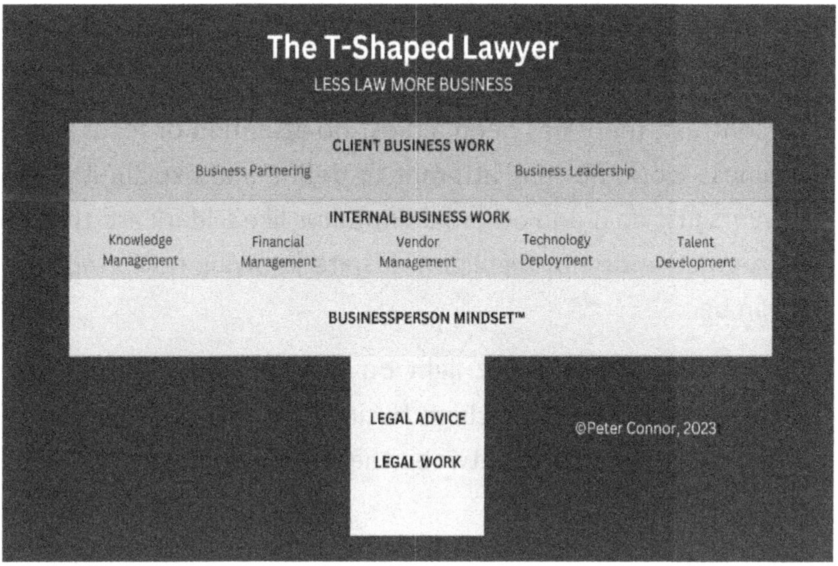

A. The Distinction between Internal and Client Business Work

When we think carefully about the idea of business work, it soon becomes apparent that there are two broad categories of this work that lawyers and others in legal departments and firms undertake to varying degrees:

- *Internal business work*: for the benefit of the legal department or firm
- *Client business work*: for the benefit of the business of the client organisation.

Internal business work, such as the examples shown above, has always been a focus area for firms because firms need to run as a business to maximise profits. In recent times, internal business work in legal departments, including the same examples, has attracted a lot more attention as evidenced by the rise of legal operations and the increasing number of references to 'running legal like a business'.[132]

By contrast, there has been almost no attention or focus on client business work, nor any attempt to define and explain it[133]. Some lawyers just do it and others do not. It is like a 'dark art' that those who practice do not highlight, despite knowing how empowering it can be.

Before we shine a bright light on this dark art, and discuss the meaning of internal and client business work in more detail, what is the main distinction between these two types of work and why does it matter?

At a high level, the essential difference is that, from your perspective working as a lawyer in a legal department or firm, internal business work is **inwards-focused** whereas client business work is **outward-focused**. As I explained in Chapter 3, the default vision of just aspiring to be better lawyers results in an internal or inwards focus. That partly explains[134] why there has been so much attention on internal business work in the corporate legal industry, and little to no attention on client business work.

Why does the distinction between internal and client business work matter?

Both internal business work and client business work are important because both can add value. However, **internal business work adds value predominantly for the legal department** or firm, whereas **client business work adds value to those who should matter most – your clients.**

Client business work has much more of an impact from your client's perspective because it is specifically for their benefit.

Clients rarely value or even notice the impact of internal business work.

Focusing on client business work will help you achieve what I have suggested should be your paramount change objective – adding value for your clients, not just your legal department or firm. Shifting your primary focus in this way, as an individual lawyer, legal department, or firm, changes everything.

Reframing 'the name of the game'

With the default vision and an inwards focus on internal business work, the **'name of the game' for virtually everyone in the corporate legal industry is lowering cost and enhancing efficiency of so-called 'legal service delivery'**. This is the metaphorical 'puck' that everyone is focused on.

However, if you change the vision to the one proposed in this book, you will automatically switch your primary focus:

From	To
You & your department/ firm	Your clients
An inward focus	An outward focus
Efficiency	Effectiveness
Legal service delivery	Providing outcomes clients need
Where the puck is	Where the puck is going
Internal business work	Client business work

With those introductory comments to set the scene and highlight the significance of the distinction, let's explore what each of these types of business work involve, and how they apply to in-house and law firm lawyers.

B. Internal Business Work

There are many similarities between internal business work for a legal department and internal business work for a firm, but there also some crucial differences.

Internal business work for the legal department

In recent years, internal business work for the legal department has become known as *legal operations*. I commented on this trend in Chapter 1. Legal operations, or internal business work in a legal department, is not legal work. Rather, it is business work for the legal department. It covers a wide range of work such as administrative work, financial management, knowledge management, vendor management and technology procurement, development, and deployment.

There are a few important points to highlight about this type of business work:

- in general, this work is focused on optimising the operations of the legal department especially in relation to controlling costs and enhancing efficiency.
- in smaller legal departments this work is done, often reluctantly, by lawyers or administrators.
- As the importance of this category of business work becomes increasingly recognised, legal departments have rightly elected to transfer dedicated resources from within or hire legal operations professionals to do some or all this work.

- as an alternative to hiring people to do this work, legal departments have in recent times, engaged third party consultants to do some of it. This has been one of the catalysts for the explosion of ALSPs or NewLaw businesses. As I pointed out in Chapter 1, that descriptor is largely inaccurate because, except for legal talent on demand, these businesses provide business products and services, not legal services.

How is internal business work relevant you as an in-house lawyer?

Because of the recent trends referred to above, it is often unnecessary for you, as a lawyer, to do much business work for the benefit of the legal department, unless you aspire to do more of this type of work or change into one of these non-legal roles. However, it is important that you at least understand and, where appropriate support, internal business work. This is especially important if you are, or aspire to be, in a more senior position in your firm or legal department, so that are able to manage this work.

In fact, the more senior you become, the more likely it is that you will spend less time on traditional legal work and more time on internal business work. It is for that reason that I feature internal business work in the T-Shaped Lawyer vision, and cover the capabilities required to do this work in the T-Shaped Lawyer Framework.

Is business work for the benefit of the legal department relevant to you if you work in a firm?

If you work as a lawyer in a firm, you may think that this type of business work is not relevant to you. If so, you would be mistaken, and you and the firm will miss a significant opportunity to add value for your in-house legal clients.

Legal departments have lots of needs over and above the need for legal advice. Indeed, general counsel and the leadership team often spend as much, if not more, time dealing with internal business work as they on legal advice and other legal work.

You and your firm may not have been specifically asked to help with their internal business work, however, you should try to understand that work, and either assist or offer the assistance of others in your firm or any associated ALSP business.

Example: ways in which firms may assist legal departments with their internal business work. As a lawyer in a firm, you may not be the person who provides this help yourself, but you can connect the appropriate resource in the firm to provide this help:

▪ facilitating hiring, retention, and development of the legal department	▪ arranging for back up human resources on an as needed basis	▪ assisting process improvement and project management
▪ advising on, or offering, technology solutions	▪ providing pro-active help with cost management.	▪ planning for how to address major challenges and priorities

Your client will appreciate it and will probably be amazed, as so few law firm lawyers do that. At the very least, it shows that you really care and are making a genuine attempt to understand your client. Often, this can lead to additional business revenue for the firm.

Because someone from the legal department is often the one who engages your firm, helping the legal department with their business work might be viewed as client business work. However, because the nature of this work for the legal department is very different to helping the business executives with the business of the company, it is preferable to reserve the expression 'client business work' to the latter and not use it to describe the former.

Internal business work for the law firm

Law firms have for many years recognised the importance of internal business work for the firm. Like internal business work for the legal department, internal business work for the firm is not legal work. Rather it is business work primarily to benefit the firm, not the client.[135] This work also covers administrative work, financial management, vendor management, knowledge management, talent development and technology deployment. However, because a firm is a profit-making business, internal business work for a firm extends to other areas especially marketing and business development.

Most of the general comments made above, in relation to internal business work for a legal department, apply equally to internal business work for a firm. That said, long before legal departments started focusing on legal operations, firms hired a range of non-legal professionals to do a wide range of this work such as general management, business development, human resource, marketing, technology, and knowledge management.

Again, a lawyer working in a firm will rarely spend much time doing internal business work. However, if you are, or aspire to be, a partner in the firm, then you should at least understand what this work is because it is central to the optimal operation of the business of the firm.

The one area of internal business work that you, as a lawyer, should be significantly involved in, is business development. Why? Because business development is primarily about relationships, and typically, it is you as the lawyer, who has the main relationship with someone from the legal department. Below is a very brief commentary on business development work.

Business development

If you work in a firm, then your legal work is obviously extremely important. However, being good at legal work alone will rarely lead to a successful career in a firm. Business development is, arguably, as critical to your success.

Business development is a vast topic beyond the scope of this book. There are various detailed resources available on this topic[136]. For present purposes, the following brief overview highlights what business development work is, and why it is another important example of business work relevant to lawyers.

What is business development and why is it important?

Business development is the ability to create long term value for your firm by identifying and executing business enhancement opportunities. The most obvious form of business development in a firm is the ability to attract new clients and/or new legal work from existing clients.

But there are other new, and less obvious, forms of business development. The business of firms was once limited to providing legal advice and doing legal work. Now, progressive firms are starting to provide a range of business services – such as legal operations consulting and managed services – and products to clients. That is **because client legal departments do not just have legal problems; they have business problems**. As such, business development is now as much about identifying new and different ways to help clients with their business, as it is about expanding the provision of legal services.

You could say that the goal of business development for lawyers in firms is to become **trusted advisors** to, at least, your most important clients. If you have succeeded in becoming a trusted advisor, then your client will see you as a 'go-to' resource not just for legal counsel, but for input on a range of business issues. Attaining trusted advisor status entrenches your relationship with your client, and often allows you to identify new revenue streams. You do not usually become a trusted advisor purely based on the quality and responsiveness of your legal services. Rather, you earn that status if you have business smarts, and if you can provide sound business input, in addition to legal advice. This point is reinforced later in this chapter by reference to the authoritative book *The Trusted Advisor*.

There are other aspects to running and growing the business of a firm that involve business, not just legal, work. This includes attracting, retaining, and developing talent; increasing lawyer utilisation and profitability; identifying strategic partnerships and new revenue streams; and expanding into new geographic and practice areas.

Larger firms often retain a range of specialists to help them in these areas, however, at least, the partners of a firm should understand and be able to lead the development of the business in these areas.

Is business development relevant to in-house lawyers?

Most in-house lawyers will view business development as only relevant to those working in a firm. However, business development is relevant to an in-house lawyer in several ways:

- As 'the client', you can and should influence the business development activities of law firms although your probably rarely do that.

  In-house lawyers regularly express their disappointment to me that law firm business development typically consists of just an invitation to lunch or the standard notification of a legal update. You are the buyer, and as such, you can and should be more creative and direct about what you would like to receive from the firms that you use or are thinking about using. Firms are willing to go to great lengths to offer 'free' or so called 'value added' products or services, under the umbrella of business development.

  Example: firms have been known to host hackathons or to collaborate on various projects.

  Firms may not initiate efforts to help your legal department with internal business work, but you may be able to facilitate that happening under the guise of business development.

- As we will discuss below, helping to identify, create and implement business opportunities for your company is what business partnering and business leadership is all about. Isn't that a form of business development for the company that you work for?

  In-house lawyers have not historically thought of business development as relevant to them,[137] however, that may change if you accept and embrace the T-Shaped Lawyer vision that I am advocating.

My intention in defining and explaining internal business work for legal departments and firms is not to provide comprehensive or exhaustive coverage. That would involve an entire book or series of books. My primary aim is to clarify the meaning of internal business work. Now that I have done that, you should have a reasonable level of understanding about business development, legal operations, legal technology, and other topics related to internal business work. If you want to find out more about this type of work, there are an ever-increasing number of resources readily available, because this work attracts so much attention.

The other reason why I have not gone into greater detail about internal business work is because **doing** this type of work is not something that is crucial to becoming a T-Shaped Lawyer. It will generally be sufficient for you, as a lawyer, to **understand** and **support** this type of work because it will typically be done by others in your legal department or firm. That said, it is important enough to warrant inclusion in the T-Shaped Lawyer vision and coverage in the T-Shaped Lawyer Framework.

What is crucial to becoming a T-Shaped Lawyer is doing **client business work**. Internal business work may help you to add more value for your legal department or firm. However, it is client business work that will help you achieve the paramount change objective of adding more value **for your clients**[138]. You will struggle to find anything that clearly defines and describes client business work. That is what the rest of the book will focus on.

C. Client Business work

Client business work is work or services, other than any legal work, that is specifically for the benefit of business of your client.[139]

There are a few points worth highlighting about this high-level definition:

- Legal advice and other types of legal work are for the benefit of the client, but that is not included in the definition of client business work.
- 'For the benefit of the business of your client' means objectively, in the best interests of the organisation. In most cases, those interests will align with the interests of the individual executives with whom you may interact. However, when those interests conflict, then the interests of the organisation prevail[140].
- As mentioned earlier, I prefer not to use the expression *client* to describe the business and functional executives to whom an in-house lawyer provides services. However, the reason that I have chosen to use the expression *client business work* is because client is a widely understood concept in the

corporate legal industry, and it is does accurately describe the beneficiary of this type of business work.

To fully understand what I mean by client business work, it is necessary to be more specific than the high-level definition above.

In broad terms, client business work involves helping to solve or prevent business problems and to create or optimise business opportunities.

There are two subcategories of client business work:

- **Business Partnering** which involves the provision of **business input and advice** that typically does not involve a lot of additional time; and
- **Business Leadership** which involves investing time to do **business work** that goes above and beyond business input and advice, and typically involves project work.

Before we examine these two categories of client business work in detail in the next two chapters, it is worth pointing out that, in addition to all the reasons already advanced for doing client business work, there is one more reason that will resonate with most corporate lawyers – the desire to be a trusted advisor.

D. Becoming a Trusted Advisor

Most corporate lawyers would say that they aspire to become a *'trusted advisor'* at least to their most important clients. The reason is obvious. If you are a trusted advisor to your clients, then it is confirmation that they value you, and that your relationship with them is less transactional and more deeply entrenched.

But what does it mean to be a trusted advisor and how do you become one?

Can you become a trusted advisor to a business executive purely based on the quality of your legal advice and legal work? As a law firm lawyer, can you become a trusted advisor to an in-house lawyer client based just on excellence in the law?

Almost certainly not, in both cases.

High quality legal advice and work is the absolute minimum standard expected of all lawyers. However, becoming a trusted advisor requires much more than that.

One of the best compliments I received during my career as an in-house lawyer was when my primary senior business contact told me that he would have me on his management team even if I was not a member of the legal department and even if he had to pay for it out of his own budget. We sometimes discussed legal matters, but most of our conversations had nothing to do with the law and everything to do with a wide range of strategic and tactical business issues such as personnel challenges, organisation structure, new market strategies, alliances with third parties, pricing questions and distribution issues. I would participate in management meetings as an equal member of the management team, and provide input on any topic, not just legal matters. Outside those meetings, he would talk to me several times a day just to 'bounce' his ideas off me, or to seek my opinion on some situation or proposal. I would also proactively provide him with comments and ideas about a range of business situations. I had become his *'go-to'* person which, when you think about it, is really what being a trusted advisor is all about.

But don't just take my word for it. *The Trusted Advisor*[141], the widely recognised leading authority on this topic, confirms what I have stated above. It provides a detailed explanation of what it means to be a trusted advisor – as highlighted in the graphic below - and why becoming one is so compelling. It offers excellent tips to help you become a trusted advisor, many of which are also relevant to becoming a T-Shaped Lawyer.

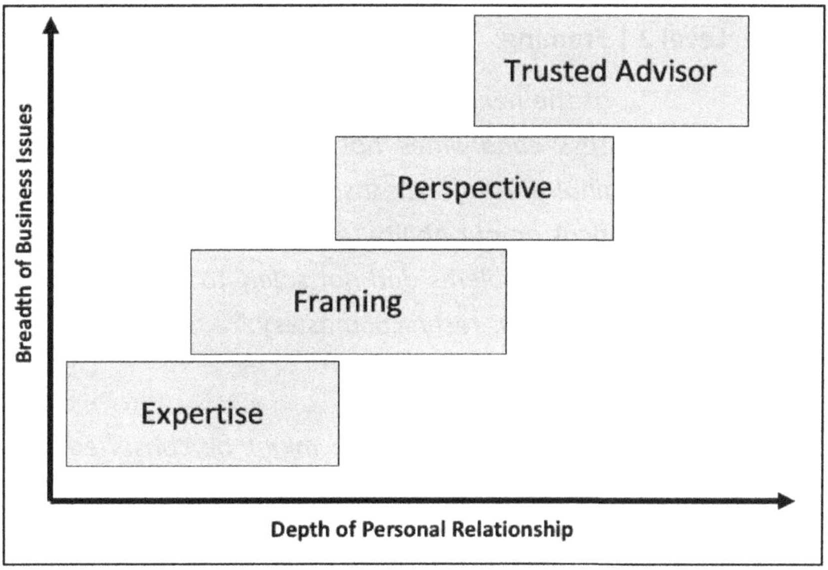

Source: The Trusted Advisor Fig 2.1, Accessed October 24, 2023. **Note that the vertical axis shows increasing importance of business involvement as progress from expert to trusted advisor.**

The book outlines the 4 different possible levels that describe the relationships that advisory professionals, including lawyers, typically have with their clients as shown above:

1. **Level 1 | Expertise**:

The first level, and the relationship most professionals have with their clients, is of an expert.

> "'*We may perform with excellence and expertise, but our activities are limited in scope. As this expertise-based role increasingly gets moved on-line and somewhat automated, the criticality of the next levels (of relationship) rises."*

2. **Level 2 | Framing**:

> *"... at the next level the client may sense that we possess capabilities not directly related to our original area of expertise. Additionally, we begin to focus on our ability to define (and solve) more general problems and not solely to give answers based on our technical mastery."*

3. **Level 3 | Perspective**:

> *"... at the third level we might be consulted on broad strategy issues related to our specific expertise, but not limited only to that expertise. We are no longer seen through the client's eyes as having just technical expertise or problem definition and problem-solving abilities, but we are seen as a valued resource in terms of our ability to put issues in context and to provide perspective. We begin to offer advice proactively and to identify issues in their organisational context."*

4. **Level 4 | Trusted Advisor**:

> *"... the highest level, the pinnacle, is that of a trusted advisor, in which virtually all issues, personal and professional, are open to discussion and exploration. The trusted advisor is the person the client turns to when an issue first arises, often in times of great urgency: a crisis, a change, a triumph, or a defeat."*

There are a few points worth highlighting about this explanation of the concept of a trusted advisor that are very relevant to this book:

- The relationship that most lawyers have with most of their clients could be categorised as Level 1, based on legal expertise, and sometimes as Level 2. This categorisation corresponds closely with the I-shaped lawyer – an expert but not an expert generalist.
- Despite what many lawyers may believe, they are not trusted advisors to their clients.
- Becoming a trusted advisor to anyone (Level 4) is an extremely rare and special relationship, and the expression should only be used to describe a relationship of the kind defined above in the book.
- It is only realistic to aspire to this sort of relationship with just your most important and regular clients.
- As the authors point out in the book, at least initially,

  > *"... most of our daily professional lives are spent operating at levels 1 and 2; relatively little of our time is spent actually working at levels 3 and 4.*

> *The issue is not hours in a day, but rather the ability to shift instantly and with ease at any level when necessary."*

The authors of *The Trusted Advisor* confirm, without any shadow of a doubt, that pure excellence in the law will not suffice to become a trusted advisor to any client. To achieve that lofty goal, it is imperative to move beyond the law and to become a businessperson who provides business input and advice, not just legal advice, and does business work, not just legal work for the benefit of the client, not just your legal department or firm.

In other words, if you want to become a trusted advisor to any of your clients it is essential that you become a T-Shaped Lawyer as defined in this book.

To sum up, internal business work is important and is something that a T-Shaped Lawyer needs to at least understand and support. However, **it is doing client business work, over and above legal work, that is really at the heart of my proposed new vision of a T-Shaped Lawyer.** This vision applies to both lawyers working in firms and to those working in-house, but it is applicable in slightly different ways as explained in the next two chapters.

CHAPTER 6

BUSINESS PARTNERING

I started advocating for business partnering in 2004, when I wrote an article on the topic for in-house lawyers published in the Association of Corporate Counsel's Docket Magazine[142]. Since then, I have talked to thousands of in-house and law firm lawyers around the world about business partnering and their reactions are many and varied, including those who:

- have never heard of the expression and who are often hesitant to do it.
- mistakenly confuse it with being a business partner, and sometimes, as a result, do not like the expression.
- rate it as the top priority for themselves and for other lawyers in their team or firm.

A. What is Business Partnering and how is it different to being a business partner?

Most lawyers, and most commentators, refer to business partnering as '*understanding the business and developing strong working relationships with our business clients*'.

That could be a definition of being a business partner. **But business partner is a noun, business partnering is a verb.**

Business partnering is not something you are. It is something you do.

You can be a business partner, as many in-house lawyers are, but not engage in business partnering at all. To put it another way, if you are business partner, it means you probably have a 'seat at the table'[143], but business partnering focuses on what you do when you are `at the table'. Being a business partner is a necessary, but not sufficient, condition to engage in business partnering.

Business partnering applies to in-house lawyers and to lawyers working in firms, but it applies in different ways, primarily because of the relative proximity to those working in the business of the corporation. I will try to indicate when a comment applies to one group but not the other.

So, what do I mean by business partnering?

Business partnering is helping to solve or prevent business problems and to create or optimise business opportunities <u>by providing business input or business advice to your clients.</u>

There are several general points that I want to highlight to explain this idea in more detail before I focus on a few specific points that are especially important:

- Examples of business input or advice include:

▪ decision support: see discussion below for more detail	▪ clarifying the business objectives	▪ commenting on a business discussion in a meeting or by email
▪ raising potential	▪ suggesting alternative	▪ pointing out non-legal risks

business issues with a proposal	ways to achieve a better business outcome	especially reputational risks
▪ identifying a business opportunity	▪ anticipating a business problem	▪ referring to another analogous business situation
▪ connecting one colleague with another who has relevant input	▪ highlighting a personnel, resource, or process problem	▪ recommending a course of action

- The business input or advice may be, and typically is, provided in conjunction with legal advice. In fact, it may be difficult to separate the two. However, if you have business input to offer, you can and should do so, even if there is no legal issue involved.
- **Providing business-oriented, pragmatic legal advice is something you want to do as a lawyer but that is not, as many people believe, business partnering**.
- Giving business- oriented legal advice is completely different to providing business input and business advice. As mentioned above, business oriented legal advice may be mixed with

business advice when it is delivered to a client, however, it is preferable not to mix the two ideas when discussing it conceptually because it can be confusing to lawyers who have not previously focused on offering business advice.

- **That is why it is important to reserve the expression *business partnering* only to the provision of business input or business advice**.
- Usually, this kind of business input or advice can be done without taking much, if any, additional time on your part. You can do it during a meeting, a conference call, or an email exchange that you are already involved in.
- Efforts to help your clients with business problems and opportunities that involve more than a brief piece of advice or input, and do involve considerable time on your part, are typically more appropriately categorised as *business leadership*, as explained in the next chapter.
- As an in-house lawyer, when you engage in business partnering, you work together with one or more of your work colleagues from other functions such as sales, finance engineering and human resources. As such, the concept of partnering is appropriate because, although you all work for the same organisation, you are in different functions and have different roles. However, where business partnering works best is when you engage with your colleagues as equals, a position that you will need to earn, typically through your words and actions, and not demand as a right.
- Business input may be provided in many different forms – it could be as simple as asking a question, making a suggestion,

highlighting some consequences, or it could involve a specific recommendation.

- Deciding when, where and how to communicate business input is something that should be adapted to the context and your unique circumstances.
- Business input or advice can be strategic, but it often is tactical and operational especially when you first start focusing on it.
- Lawyers often think, and speak, of themselves as problem-solvers, which of course, is admirable. But business partnering involves more than that. It involves a focus on preventing, not just solving, problems. It also involves a focus on opportunities, *n*ot just implementing opportunities but also helping to identify, create, and optimise them.

Below are two specific questions that I am often asked to clarify.

B. <u>Does Business Partnering Involve Making Business Decisions?</u>

As I have highlighted above, decision support is a classic example of business partnering. The word 'support' here is key. Providing business input and advice to your clients **does not involve you making a business decision for them**. Typically, making a business decision, unless it relates to purely internal business work, extends beyond your area of responsibility or authority. However, there is absolutely nothing stopping you from supporting a business executive to make an optimal business decision that is within their area of responsibility or authority.

Reminding yourself that all you are doing in business partnering is offering business input or business advice, not making the ultimate decision, provides a kind of 'safe harbour' for you to engage in this type of client business work.

Pointing out to clients that you are only providing advice, not making the decision, is sometimes necessary when a client tries to obtain a 'legal sign off' on a business decision as a form of insurance in case something goes wrong later. If this happens to you, then you should make it clear that any advice you offer, whether of a legal or business nature, should not be misinterpreted as you making the business decision to proceed.

Having said that, in the absence of such a blatant 'legal sign off' situation, it is generally preferable not to highlight the fact that you are only offering advice and that the executive needs to make the decision. The reason is because business partnering works best, and you maximise your chances of having a close professional relationship with an executive when the executive feels as if you are jointly making the decision and sharing the responsibility.

Now you might say, *'but I don't want to be responsible for a bad business decision'*. This may be a theoretical 'risk' with business partnering but in practise, I have never heard of a lawyer who suffered adverse consequences purely[144] because they provided business advice in relation to a matter where the business outcome was suboptimal. The reason for that is probably because, although you may have made the executive *feel as if* you are making the decision 'together', they know, and others know, that you are not actually making the decision. To put in another way, because business decision making is outside your authority as a lawyer, ultimate responsibility for that decision rests with the executive, not with you.[145]

All the above is not to say that lawyers do not make decisions. You do.

Example: Lawyers need to decide what stance to take on legal issues and legal advice. Lawyers in management positions also need to make internal business decisions in relation to the legal department or firm, such as where to spend money, who to hire and who to engage to help them.

However, unlike the business decisions referred to above, these decisions are within the legal department or firm's scope of responsibility and authority.

As a lawyer, you may make decisions in relation to legal work or internal business work. However, other than that, it is important to remember that you do not make business decisions for your client. You only offer business input or business advice to help your clients make optimal decisions.

Decision-making is a crucial competency for lawyers because, although the scope for actual business decision making may be limited to legal and internal business work, it becomes very relevant and useful when providing client business decision support to corporate executives. That is why decision-making is a T-Shaped Lawyer Framework competency and covered in the second book.

C. How Do You Become a Business Partner and Who is Your Client?

I mentioned earlier that being a business partner is not the same thing as engaging in business partnering. However, to do that effectively, it is important to be a business partner or, as some like to say, have `a seat at the table'. Simply put, you need to have the opportunity to interact with the business executives, to provide them with business advice or input. How should you create those opportunities?

If you work in a law firm or are a junior in-house lawyer, then you may have little to no direct interaction with business executives. That can make it difficult for you to establish direct business partner relationships. However, there is generally nothing stopping you from providing business advice and input to an executive when you do have the opportunity, or to an in-house lawyer who does have the regular connection with the executive.

Most in-house lawyers will naturally have these opportunities because they support a business or functional group. Opportunities arise to engage in business partnering arise when executives from that group approach you for legal advice. If there is a management team, then ideally the lawyer should be on that team, or at least attend the management meetings.

Do you need to be friends, or socialise, with these executives? How close do you need to be?

It is not necessary for you be friends with these executives and to socialise with them outside of a work context, to be a business partner. I rarely did this in my career as a lawyer. I preferred to maintain some separation of my work life and my personal life. Creating that separation may make it easier for some to maintain their independence and discharge their professional responsibilities as a lawyer.

That said, I think it is important to be friendly, or at least personable, with all executives, and in general, to network and socialise in a work context when you can[146].

There are some who suggest that there is a danger in lawyers getting 'too close' to their clients. They suggest that getting too close to executives, makes it difficult for lawyers to honour their professional duties as a lawyer.[147]

This view fails to appreciate the realities of how to work effectively as an in-house lawyer, and the distinctions made above. It is simply not practical, or desirable, for in-house lawyers to 'distance themselves' from the executives that they support, or to stay in some kind of 'legal bubble or cocoon'.

It may not be necessary to be **personally close** to be a business partner, and this may be what those who espouse this view are really talking about. However, it is essential that you be **professionally close** to the executives that you interact with the most, and especially with those that you wish to be a trusted advisor. By professionally close I mean to spend time with these executives so that they are willing to talk to you, not just about tasks, matters and transactions, but also about their professional challenges, motivations, priorities, and objectives.

If you do not do that, how is it possible for you to provide pragmatic business-oriented legal advice, let alone engage in business partnering?

Being a business partner involves you being professionally close to at least the executives that you interact with most often, so that you understand what they are working on and trying to achieve. **Business partnering, in simple terms, primarily involves you helping your clients, and their teams, to do their job well and to achieve their business objectives**.

Business partnering, for practical purposes, means that your client is the relevant business or functional executive.

But wait a minute, isn't my client the company, not the individual executives?

Strictly speaking your client is the company, however, because a company is a legal entity, in the real world, you interact with natural people who represent the company – the business and functional executives. In almost all cases, there will be alignment between what these executives are trying to do and the best interests of the company. As such, it is reasonable and appropriate for you to help them achieve their business objectives.

The only situation where it will not be appropriate for you to help them do what they are proposing to do, is where that is not in the best interests of the company. In that situation, you are obliged, as a lawyer, to not assist them and to take steps to escalate the matter if you are not able to dissuade the executive from proceeding. This situation, and the challenges with complying with this obligation, can apply whether you are a business partner or engage in business partnering or not.

Fortunately, this situation of a conflict between the interests of individual executives and the company rarely arises in practice in most organisations. However, when it does happen, and the lawyers either help the executives or turn a 'blind eye', it attracts a lot of attention once it becomes public knowledge, especially if there are significant adverse consequences of the business actions.

D. Business Partnering for In-House and Law Firm Lawyers Compared

Business partnering for in-house lawyers

Obviously as an in-house lawyer you have an advantage over lawyers who work in a firm when it comes to helping the business. There are a few reasons for this:

- You have more regular contact with a wider group of business and functional colleagues.
- In the course of your work, you often have a visibility to all parts of the business.
- It is easier for you to develop a deep understanding of the business.

The chance to engage more often in business partnering is one of the primary reasons that lawyers move from a firm to work in-house.

Ben Heineman, the eminent former general counsel of General Electric, summed it up nicely when he said,

> *'(The in-house role) involves not just dealing with past problems, but charting future courses; not just playing defence, but playing offense; not just providing legal advice, but being part of the business team."*[148]

Business partnering for lawyers working in a firm

If you are a lawyer working in a firm, you may not have the opportunity to engage in business partnering with the business as frequently as an in-house lawyer. However, when you do have that opportunity, you can and should do so, as outlined above. You may not be specifically asked to do so, but usually the business, and even the in-house lawyer, client will appreciate it if you have some useful business input. Indeed, a common complaint from in-house lawyers is that the advice they receive from law firms is too legalistic, not commercial and does not include a recommended course of action.

If you have adopted a Businessperson Mindset and applied this to the business of your clients, then almost every time you are working on a transaction or matter, presents an opportunity to engage in business partnering when you have some useful business advice or input to contribute.

Business partnering for government lawyers

Typically, government lawyers do not support a commercial business but rather the business of running a government department. In this case, the concept of business partnering can still be applied quite literally to supporting that business. This would include decision support and other ways to solve or prevent problems, and create and optimise opportunities for the department, by offering input and advice that extends beyond legal advice.

Business partnering, as outlined earlier, typically involves business input or advice that does not involve much, if any, additional time for you. As such, there is nothing stopping every lawyer from ramping up your business partnering activities immediately.

However, if you wish to add even more value for your client organisation, then sometimes, it may be necessary to do client business work that does involve more time commitment on your part. I refer to this type of business work as **business leadership** as explained in the next chapter.

CHAPTER 7

BUSINESS LEADERSHIP

In the process of being interviewed for the Sun Microsystems Business Leadership Award, the company's executive management made it very clear to me what they wanted from their lawyers. Being a competent lawyer was a given and nothing more than an 'admission ticket' to work for the company. They told me that they wanted more people who are ***'able to identify a business problem or opportunity and willing to do something about it, even if it was outside their job description'***. I am certain that the senior management of any company that you work with, or for, would have a very similar view.

Does that view of business leadership sounds familiar? Remember the Deloitte Insights article on the Future of Work that I cited earlier in the book? That article stated that the objective of work for everyone should be **identifying and addressing unforeseen problems and opportunities**. In other words, what might qualify as leadership today, because it is rarely done on a regular basis, may, in the future, just become the way we all work.

Let me summarise and reemphasise the statements above.

Business leadership is not only aligned with what the executive leadership team of companies see as exemplary. It is also aligned with what the experts are predicting will be the Future of Work.

A. What is Business Leadership and How is it Different to Business Partnering?

Like business partnering, business leadership involves helping to prevent and solve business problems, and to identify and implement business opportunities. But whereas business partnering involves providing business input and advice, business leadership involves going one step further, and spending time working on the problem or opportunity.

The table below summarises the main differences between a typical business partnering and a typical business leadership activity.

BUSINESS PARTNERING	BUSINESS LEADERSHIP
Business input and advice	Business work
No extra time required	Can involve significant time
Reactive	Proactive
One-on-one	Collaborating with many
Common sense paramount	Various non-traditional capabilities
Tactical/transaction focus	Strategic/not transaction specific
Some impact	Significant impact
Leadership not essential	Leadership critical

You could say that business partnering, and business leadership are just two ends of a spectrum of different ways that lawyers can do client business work to add more value for clients.

At one end of the spectrum is business partnering, that can be easily incorporated into your current ways of working by providing business input, with little to no additional time required. It can be done during an interaction with one of your clients, and you can largely rely on your common sense and your existing business partnering assets. As such, even the newest or most junior lawyer can engage in business partnering immediately.

At the other end of the spectrum, business leadership can involve a significant amount of extra work and time on your part. The good news is that there are ways to manage your time commitment in a particular project by breaking business leadership down into different levels of involvement as explained in section C below.

To better understand the meaning of business leadership, it helps to briefly outline some examples and then to highlight some key general points about business leadership.

Examples of business leadership

1. Deal Management Process (DMP)

   When Sun Microsystems broke the company up into various business units, initially the sales groups for each unit did not coordinate their activities very well. One unit would often agree business terms with a key strategic customer that would be indirectly, or in some cases directly, disadvantageous to the other units and the company. My team and I took the initiative in our region to establish a process, and to create and lead a cross business unit / functional team, to review deals with key customers *before* terms were agreed with the customer. This approach was then adopted by others and expanded worldwide throughout the company.

2. DRAM EU Anti-dumping duty

Sun, and other buyers of DRAM from Korean and Taiwanese suppliers, were surprised to discover that they had a significant residual duty liability because of the dumping practices of those suppliers. I formed and lead a cross-functional and global team to resolve the duty issues in each EU Member State, and to change our supply chain processes to ensure this would not happen again. I also jointly lead a cross-industry coalition to lobby for changes in the laws that gave rise to this rather peculiar exposure. In the process, I established the first European Government Affairs function for the company to work on a range of public policy issues.

3. Patents

My U.S legal colleagues at Citrix took the initiative to create a Patent Steering Committee and a process to review inventions against a set of criteria to determine whether and where patent applications should be filed. Prior to that, Legal would apply for a patent whenever a product development team requested it, whether that was appropriate or not. My colleagues then went one step further and initiated a plan to increase fees from licensing the patent portfolio to others.

Adjacency

One thing you might notice about these examples is that they are adjacent to traditional legal work. In other words, usually the areas of opportunity for business leadership will have some connection to the traditional legal work that you currently do, rather than be something completely unrelated. The key to spotting these opportunities is to have the Businessperson Mindset.

Fertile ground for lawyers to look for business leadership opportunities include:

▪ Data Governance, Cyber security and Privacy	▪ Enterprise Risk Management (ERM)	▪ Government Relations / Public Affairs / Lobbying
▪ Governance Risk Compliance (GRC)	▪ Protecting, enforcing, and commercialising intellectual property	▪ Environmental, Social and Governance (ESG)
▪ Sustainability	▪ Corporate Culture – ethics	▪ Innovation

The other thing to note about many business leadership opportunities is that your work can benefit both the legal department and the company.

Example: often you can use a business leadership project to influence the allocation of appropriate non-legal resources to an area so that, in future, lawyers are only involved to the extent that they should be.

Business leadership can often be a win/win scenario for the legal department and the company.

Richard Susskind, in the latest version of his book *'Tomorrow's Lawyers'*[149], suggests that firms and legal departments should adopt a mission and strategies to design processes and systems to replace current ways of working by lawyers. He also lists a series of new roles to achieve this aim such as legal design thinking, legal process analyst, legal no coder, legal data scientist and legal project manager.

There are a few things I would say in this context about this idea:

- This work is another example of business work that lawyers could do with appropriate training, although that work can, and often will, be done by others.
- If this work solely benefits the legal department or firm, then it is what I have coined internal business work.
- If, however, this work benefits the business, for example enabling the business to self-help and obtain the information or documents they need more quickly, then it qualifies as business leadership.
- To the extent that this work also frees up your time as a lawyer to do other types of business leadership work, it is an essential part of what I refer to as work rationalisation.

Silos and White Space

I am sometimes asked *'isn't business leadership doing the job of a business or functional executive at the company. Why would I want to do 'their job'?'*

As you can see from the above examples, the business work involved in business leadership almost always does not involve doing someone's job, because it does not fall into anyone's job scope. Rather, it typically falls into what has sometimes been described as *'white space'*[150] in an organisation. White space is the gap that exists in most organisations and sits between the vertical functional silos. No-one realises it is there, unless and until something 'falls between the cracks'; something important is not progressing; or somebody steps up and ventures outside of their siloed area of responsibility to get involved.

Frankly, even if it did involve doing something that somebody else should do, why wouldn't you get involved if it is important enough? In this situation, you might have to be more sensitive about how you get involved.

'No Go' client business work that you should NOT be doing

Having said that, and just to be clear, business leadership is not about doing any business work done by clients just because they are incompetent or because you believe you can do it better.

Example: reviewing marketing or advertising copy. It may or may not be appropriate for you to review this copy to see if there are any legal issues. However, if you do believe it is necessary for you to do so, then in some cases, lawyers just end up re-writing the copy, not just to remove legal issues, but also to improve it. Whilst it may be true that you can do their job better than they can do it, and *'It's just easier if I do it'*, that is not a reason for you to do this business work.

This type of work is what I refer to as 'No Go' client business work and is NOT what I mean by business leadership or business partnering. You must be selective about the type of client business work that you opt to do, and only do something if it contributes significant value to the company and no-one else is doing it.

B. Business Leadership for In-House and Law Firm Lawyers Compared

Business leadership for in-house lawyers

If you are an in-house lawyer, then you are usually uniquely placed to do business leadership work.

First, your traditional work means that you have a broad and deep visibility across the company in a way that your non-legal colleagues, and even senior management, do not have. That means that you are more likely to identify current and unseen business problems and opportunities. It also means that you can have the understanding and network to engage in business leadership to address these.

Second, Legal is different to other functions in a company. At a very simplistic level, for example, Finance is expected to do the accounts; HR is expected to hire, develop, and fire people; Manufacturing is expected to produce products; and Sales is expected to sell products. Those expectations leave little wiggle room as far as work is concerned if you work in those parts of the business.

While Legal is expected to identify and address legal risk, unlike these other functions, **there is generally no specific deliverable expected from Legal**. As such you are not burdened by senior management's expectation of you always doing specific work.

Most of the work that in-house lawyers do results not from a management expectation or directive, but rather from an explicit or implicit decision by Legal that this work is necessary[151].

As I say to my clients,

'the only limitation on in-house lawyers doing new work is your imagination, the appetite for risk and the way you have always worked.'

No doubt this statement will shock and horrify many lawyers. However, when you think carefully about my comment, you will realise that lawyers working in legal departments have a lot more freedom than they think, to change their current work and to do new work. That freedom is critical to aggressively use a work rationalisation methodology, as you must, to not only cope with current workloads but also free up time so that you can spend more time on business leadership work.

Finally, some legal departments have turned themselves from cost centres into profit centres by charging third parties for their services. Whilst this may be an opportunity for some legal departments, this is not an essential aspect of business leadership. Indeed, as you can see from the examples above, business leadership work may, in some cases, lead directly to new revenue for the company but in many cases, it does not.

Business leadership for law firm lawyers

As a lawyer working in a firm, you do not usually enjoy the above advantages. Also, you do not typically have the same proximity to the business and functional executives or the business in general.

Clearly the scope for you to engage in business leadership is not the same as it is for an in-house lawyer.

However, like in-house lawyers, you are well trained to anticipate problems and opportunities that others may not see. Unlike in-house lawyers, you have the advantage that you, or your law firm colleagues, may well see similar problems and opportunities for other clients. Drawing on that experience, combined with resources that are often available to firms but not to in-house teams, may enable you to identify, and in some cases help design and/or implement, solutions for business clients to these current and unforeseen problems and opportunities.

In short, with a Businessperson Mindset and an understanding of business leadership and how critically important it can be, there is still considerable scope for law firm lawyers to do business leadership work typically, in conjunction with any in-house lawyers.

C. <u>Levels of Business Leadership: A Multi-Phased Approach</u>

As the authors of *Trusted Advisor* explained,

> *"... most of our daily professional lives are spent operating at levels 1 and 2; relatively little of our time is spent actually working at levels 3 and 4 (as a trusted advisor). The issue is not hours in a day, but rather the ability to shift instantly and with ease at any level when necessary."*

So too with business leadership. Opportunities to show business leadership do not come along every day. It may be that for some period, you are only doing business partnering, in addition to legal advice and work, and not doing any business leadership work. The point is that you know what to look for and are ready to act, as and when the opportunities arise.

Also, business leadership is not a 'one size fits all', 'all or nothing' concept. As shown below, it is possible to vary the extent to which you engage in business leadership according to your unique situation at any time. This can take into account, for example, your seniority, time working with or for the organisation, level of relationships with key executives, and your available time.

Business Leadership Levels of involvement

LEVEL	CONTRIBUTION
1	Identify & escalate business problem or opportunity
2	Suggest solution or process to reach solution
3	Influence others to support solution or process
4	Take steps to implement solution or initiate process
5	Lead efforts to form a project team
6	Participate as member of project team
7	Lead the project team

If you are just starting your career, or for other reasons, it may be that you have limited time to engage in business leadership. However, even if you only have time to go to the first stage above, identifying and escalating a business problem or opportunity, that represents business leadership. The more time you can devote to business leadership projects, the further down the above list you can go, the more value you can add for your business clients.

I use the expression Business Leadership to describe this work because, unlike business partnering, one of the essential requirements as you progress into the higher levels outlined above, is leadership. You want to be able to influence others, who typically, are not lawyers and do not report to you, to support your initiative and ideas.

It is important to note that business leadership is different to general leadership. It is not about leading the legal department, it is about leading the business and making a significant impact on the business. The more you understand the business, the more you will identify business leadership opportunities and the more you will be able to contribute.

There are many ways to become better at business partnering and business leadership. These are outlined in the T-Shaped Lawyer Framework in the second book. However, one book worth mentioning at this stage, to help you to be better at business leadership, is *Upstream: How to Solve Problems Before They Happen.*[152]

The central idea in the book is that you want to try to avoid doing downstream work – reacting to problems – and, instead, do more upstream work – trying to solve problems before they arise. This is precisely the kind of work I am talking about when I refer to identifying and addressing unseen problems and opportunities. The book proposes some specific ideas for how to stop being dragged downstream, and how to do upstream work.

Finally, and **perhaps counterintuitively for some, doing client business work also helps your traditional legal work and the provision of legal advice**. In my experience, the business is more likely to share more information with you about their plans, and at an earlier stage, if they see you as a 'member' of the business team. Then you often have an opportunity to spot any legal or ethical issues and, because of your enhanced relationship with the business, influence the decision before it is too late. This partly responds to some concerns about doing client business work which we shall now discuss in more detail in the next chapter.

CHAPTER 8

ADDRESSING COMMON CONCERNS WITH CLIENT BUSINESS WORK

I have proposed the T-Shaped Lawyer vision in workshops all over the world to literally thousands of corporate lawyers over the last 8 years or so. The reactions to this idea of being a businessperson, not just a lawyer, and doing client business work covers a full spectrum.

At one end of the spectrum are those who say this is nothing new, it is what they have been doing for years. That is true in some cases, but typically these lawyers do it less than they think. More importantly, they do not call it out or spell it out to others – something I hope they will do now after reading this book.

At the other end of the spectrum are those who are very uncomfortable with the idea and find any number of reasons why they believe they cannot do client business work, or they would prefer to just stick to doing legal work.

Ultimately, of course, it is your choice.

That said, I want to identify and address the common concerns because often they are based on a misunderstanding or misconception.

Does being a T-Shaped Lawyer conflict with your 'professional obligations as a lawyer'?

The most serious concern that is raised is that being a businessperson as well as a lawyer, wearing 'two hats', or doing client business work somehow results in a conflict with your professional duties or obligations as a lawyer. The explicit or implicit inference is that is 'better' or 'safer' to not get 'too close' to the business executives, just `stay in your legal lane', stick to being a lawyer, and just do legal work and provide legal advice.

At first glance, you may think that there is some merit in these statements. However, let's examine these claims in more detail and remember that it is important to be precise.

Lawyers do have professional duties that are not applicable to other corporate employees.

These duties include duties to the court, duties to the client, and duties to obey the law. Do these duties sometimes raise difficult issues for corporate lawyers, especially in-house lawyers? Of course, they do, and there are a few high-profile cases[153] where the lawyers involved did not discharge their professional duties as they should.

However, this challenge for corporate lawyers applies whether you are trying to be a T-Shaped Lawyer or not. Indeed, when you examine those cases in detail, it is evident that the failing of each lawyer did not arise because the lawyer was too close to the executives or trying to give business advice. Rather it was a case of the lawyer, for different reasons, succumbing to pressure from executives and failing to do what was patently in the best interests of the company, or what was required by the law. Being able to deal with inappropriate pressure from executives, and being able to distinguish between what is the right and the wrong thing to do, is something that every lawyer must be capable of doing.

That said, there are two specific duties that are most often cited as being difficult for lawyers to comply with, if you try to be a businessperson as well as a lawyer, and if you offer business advice and do business work:

- the duty to be independent[154] and to provide independent legal advice to the client.
- the duty to act ethically and to call out unethical client conduct.

A. <u>Independence</u>

The comment sometimes made is how can you be independent when you are trying to be close to the business executives and engage in business discussions?

My own experience, and that of many other lawyers, has shown that it is easily possible to comply with the requirement to maintain independence despite being close to the business executives and helping them with their work. The following points might help to put your mind at rest about this perceived issue of independence:

- Typically, the requirement to be independent does not mean maintaining a siloed legal department within the corporation, separation from the executives and/or adopting formal ways of interacting with the executives. This is not how most legal departments operate in practise, nor is it necessary or desirable to distance yourselves from the business for reasons mentioned earlier in the book.
- The requirement to be independent usually involves avoiding a personal conflict of interest. A personal conflict

of interest could arise for a corporate lawyer but not because they are providing business advice and doing business work. If such a conflict were to manifest itself, then problems would almost always arise because of the legal advice that was, or should have been, provided, not any business advice.

- The other aspect of the requirement to be independent is being able to resist any influence or pressure by business executives to do the 'wrong thing' or to not provide honest independent legal advice. The general counsel reporting up through the CEO, or to the Board, certainly helps this aspect of independence. Does trying to get close to the business, and providing business advice and doing business work to help them, make it more difficult to resist such pressure? There is no logical reason for that to be the case. On the contrary, being close to the business and the business executives generally, makes it easier to resist such pressure as explained below.

B. The Ability to Act Ethically and to Provide Ethical Guidance

Some people question how you, as a lawyer, can call out illegal or unethical behaviour of business executives if you have a close relationship with them as an equal member of the business team. According to this line of argument, the fact that a few lawyers did not do the right thing in some few high-profile cases means that lawyers should not get too close to the business and should just stick to being lawyers and just doing legal work and nothing else.[155]

There are several points to be made in response to this argument:

- If a business executive wants to do the wrong thing, they will do so whether they have a close relationship with their in-house lawyer or not, and whether the lawyer sticks to just doing law or also provides business advice and does business work.
- While in almost all cases, helping the business by providing business advice and doing business work involves helping business executives, if the interests of an executive and the client corporation diverge, then the lawyer's allegiance is to the corporation not the executive. It is difficult to imagine a situation where Illegal or unethical behaviour will ever be in the corporation's long-term best interests, and this should give the lawyer the confidence to try to influence the outcome or to escalate it, however difficult this may be.
- Most in-house lawyers develop close professional relationships with their non-legal colleagues without any problem whatsoever.
- Being close to the business and to key business executives:
    - helps lawyers provide more business-oriented legal advice as well as gives them the opportunity to provide business advice as suggested in this book.
    - typically means that lawyers are involved at an earlier stage of business discussions, and therefore, have an opportunity to influence outcomes that are sound from a business, legal and ethical perspective, before problems arise.

  - usually means that, in the rare cases where the lawyer may need to push back against a business proposal, the relationship with the executives is robust enough to withstand the pressure and any fallout from the pushback.

- The fact that in a few cases, some in-house lawyers were not able to withstand the pressure and/or did not pushback or call out illegal or unethical behaviour, should not mean that all lawyers should always forgo the significant benefits from being close to the business and helping business executives in business work, not just legal work.

C. <u>Addressing Other Typical Concerns</u>

Below are some other common concerns with business partnering or business leadership together with a brief response to each point:

1. *inadequate 'business' subject matter expertise*

   My Response: You don't need to be an expert in, for example, marketing, sales, procurement, or product development, to offer business input into a discussion on these areas. Your initial 'edge', an ability to offer a unique perspective, derives not from your expertise in these areas but rather from what I refer to as your existing ***'business partnering assets'***.

   You have developed these assets from your legal studies and work. You use these for legal work, but they can be repurposed for business partnering. The assets include your:

▪ credibility as a lawyer	▪ common sense	▪ independence
▪ attention to detail and ability to distinguish between fact and opinion	▪ analytical skills to identify root cause	▪ interviewing and questioning skills
▪ ability to assess risks	▪ ability to negotiate favourable outcomes	▪ creativity in developing alternative solutions

2. *lawyers should just stick to what they are good at and leave business to the business experts*

   My Response: This comment is really a variation of the first point but is also an argument for continued specialisation. The reasons, in general, to be an expert generalist, rather than just a specialist, were discussed in chapter 3. Corporate lawyers, unlike some other professionals, can become business generalists relatively easily as explained in this book. The benefits from doing so, as opposed to just sticking to being a lawyer, are spelled out in chapters 2 and 3.

3. *too junior or too new*

   My Response: It is never too soon to start down the T-Shaped Lawyer road. Initially, your input may consist of nothing more than asking astute questions or 'connecting the dots' between your colleague and others who can provide relevant input. However, over time and with practice at business partnering, your level of knowledge of the business will develop to a point where you can make substantive input and even offer business advice and recommendations.

4. *clients don't ask me to do it*

   My Response: Clients rarely, if ever, ask you to do client business work[156] but when you do it, they typically value your contribution even more so than your legal work.

5. *clients don't like you doing it*

   My Response: It is true that sometimes providing business input may be perceived by some as 'treading on their patch'. In my experience, this rarely happens and is often a question of how you provide your input and when you do it. In an extreme case, you always have the option not to provide business input unless, without doing so, there might be adverse consequences for the client.

6. *professional indemnity insurance might not cover business advice*

   My Response: Most insurance policies do have a broad definition of legal services that would extend to business advice especially if that is something lawyers ordinarily offer in connection with legal services. Ironically, that should be a reason for law firm lawyers to offer business advice on a regular basis. That is, in fact, what the best law firm lawyers do in practice, because clients do not just want 'the law', they want to know your recommendations expressed in a way that business executives can understand and act upon.

Lawyers in firms have been doing this for many years without any adverse consequences. Why? Making a business recommendation or offering business advice carries very little risk in practice, because it would be difficult to imagine a situation where a client suffers loss solely because of some reasonable business advice from a lawyer. In fact, there is arguably a higher risk of a claim from a client if you do not raise an obvious business issue with a transaction or matter.

7. *jeopardises legal professional privilege*

My Response: In countries that recognise legal professional privilege, you may be worried that it will be compromised by providing business advice. For most of the work that most lawyers do especially in-house, privilege is not a relevant issue. For those lawyers who do work where it is important for the client to be able to claim privilege, then you have a few options. You can, in those situations, clearly separate your business advice from your legal advice and claim privilege, where it is possible to do so, in relation to the latter. If you wish to be even more cautious in these situations, you can engage an external counsel to provide the legal advice.

To summarise, the need to claim privilege typically only applies for most lawyers in a few cases, and when it does, you can manage the risk of losing privilege. It is not a reason to avoid providing business advice altogether.

To sum up, after many years of working with thousands of lawyers globally, I have not encountered a concern or issue that meant that a corporate lawyer could, or should, never engage in client business work as I have defined it.

The over-arching comment to any concern about doing client business work is to remember that both business partnering and business leadership are flexible concepts. You can do it is much or as little as you like. You can do it in many ways, and dial it up or dial it down, depending on the circumstances at any time.

Even if there is some risk in doing client business work, now that you understand the many benefits from doing this work in terms of client impact, fulfilment, and growth, isn't the risk of not engaging in client business work even greater?

It should be reassuring to know that thousands of lawyers all over the world, including me, have engaged in client business work without any problem. It should be telling that those who do it more regularly are typically the ones who are promoted into senior roles in legal departments and firms.

That said, don't take my word for it. Ben Heineman, the eminent former general counsel of General Electric concludes, in his book *'The Inside Counsel Revolution - Resolving the Partner-Guardian Tension'*[157], that it is possible for in-house lawyers to 'wear two hats' of being both a lawyer/guardian and a business partner.

CHAPTER 9

DOING 'LEGAL WORK'

The focus of this book is on business work for corporate lawyers because there is so little discussion or guidance on it. However, it is worth briefly discussing the topic of legal work[158]. After all, legal advice and legal work are important parts of the T-Shaped Lawyer vision as depicted by the vertical axis. Plus realising that vision involves doing less of certain types of work that is commonly perceived to be legal work so that you can do more business work of the type outlined in this book.

Ironically, although corporate lawyers are more familiar with legal work because they do it so regularly, there is also very little discussion on what it means and the implications of this for your work especially as an in-house lawyer.

A. <u>What is (and is not) 'legal work'?</u>

This is a simple question that is rarely discussed in legal departments or firms. Despite that, it is a crucial question for every lawyer, legal department, and firm to consider carefully in relation to every activity that you currently do or plan to do. Why? Because it informs whether you should do that activity as explained below.

How is 'legal work' and 'the practice of law' defined in the law?

You might think that there would be a clear and universal definition of 'legal work' in the law given that 'the practice of law' is something that, in almost all parts of the world, is reserved exclusively for qualified/certified lawyers. However, that is not the case.[159] A more confusing area of the law it would be difficult to find, and one could easily speculate as to why that is so.

Some countries and states attempt to define it in legislation and others leave it to case law. If you could make one generally applicable statement, then it might be that:

"The (law) defines legal work basically as work done by a legal practitioner, so the definition becomes somewhat circular."[160]

The main types of work that are often specifically included in the definition of legal work are:

- Giving advice or counsel to someone as to their legal rights or responsibilities or to those of others.
- Selecting, drafting, or completing legal documents or agreements that affect the legal rights of someone.
- Representing someone before an adjudicative body, including, but not limited to, preparing, or filing documents or conducting discovery; or
- Negotiating legal rights or responsibilities on behalf of somebody.

There is often an explicit or implicit exception to the restriction on the practice of law for employees, who are not qualified lawyers, doing contract related work for the sole benefit of their corporate employer. Even where this is no such exception, it is common practice in many countries for many types of 'legal work' to be done without any problem by people who are not lawyers.

Examples:

- Contract managers, paralegals, and commercial managers, who are not lawyers, regularly negotiate and redraft contracts, even complex and sometimes high value ones, for their corporate employer with minimal to no supervision by a qualified lawyer.
- Due diligence, discovery and legal research are now frequently done using technology and/or by non-legal professionals with minimal supervision by a qualified lawyer.

The fact that these exceptions are allowed or tolerated in a corporate legal context makes sense given that the stated purpose of the restriction on the practice of law is typically the protection of the general public as consumers of legal services.

To sum up, the law may arguably provide sufficient guidance on the definition of legal work for the purposes of restricting what non-lawyers can do. However, it is not that helpful for the purposes of corporate lawyers deciding what work they should be focusing on and what work they do not need to do. For that purpose, we need to come up with our own working definition. This is what we shall now attempt to do.

What is a helpful working definition of legal work?

Before we attempt to answer this question, it is helpful to highlight the following general points:

- **Despite the circular legal definitions of legal work referred to above, the fact that lawyers have historically done certain**

types of work does not mean that it is legal work in the sense that it necessarily must continue to be done by lawyers.

- Indeed, the scope of work for many in-house lawyers has expanded considerably over the years beyond what would generally be considered as legal work. One of the primary reasons for this is often a desire by these lawyers to be helpful to their non-legal colleagues and to get more involved.
- Whilst that motivation is terrific, and is something I encourage, it has contributed to a problem for most in-house lawyers. They are overwhelmed with work and must constantly look for ways to reduce their workload to not only cope, but also to do different, more impactful, work of the kind recommended in this book.
- Narrowing down the definition of legal work, is part of the process for in-house lawyers of freeing up time. It involves being selective about the work that needs to be eliminated or reduced, on the one hand, and that which needs to be increased, on the other. This work rationalisation process is briefly explained below.
- For law firms the perspective is different. Firms have a vested interest in generating as much billable work as possible. They might take a broad view of what constitutes legal work for the purpose of justifying the provision of these services to their clients. That said, it is also in a firm's interest to control costs by engaging non-legal professionals to do work that is not strictly speaking legal work.

With those points as context, what is a helpful working definition of legal work?

A useful working definition of Legal Work is <u>'work that only a qualified lawyer can do to the standard necessary in any situation.'</u>

B. <u>What 'legal work' should corporate lawyers be doing?</u>

If we apply this definition of legal work, it helps to clarify what legal work corporate lawyers should be doing at any point of time. It also helps to identify the types of work that lawyers should not be doing, and that can either be 'redesigned away', automated or done by others.

Examples:

- Applying that definition, in almost all cases, analysing and providing advice on the law would currently be best done by a qualified lawyer.
- Likewise, preparing court documents and appearing in court on a commercial dispute would constitute legal work and be best done by a qualified lawyer.
- Drafting a unique contract for a complex commercial transaction would typically constitute legal work and be best done by a qualified lawyer. However, when it comes to more routine contracts, technology and/or non-legal professionals can be used to prepare, using templates, negotiate, using playbooks, and manage the contract with minimal to no involvement of a lawyer.

The beauty of this working definition is that it is dynamic and can change with the times, as it should.

When I first started working as a lawyer, there were only a few appropriately trained and experienced professionals who are not lawyers and technology was not a viable option for many types of work. In other words, it was almost always necessary for a qualified lawyer to do a full range of work to achieve the necessary quality. Now, much of this work, such as document or contract review and preparation, is either done more efficiently by lawyers with the help of technology or, increasingly, not done by lawyers at all. Technology or non-legal professionals can do this work to a suitable standard.

One crucial implication of this definition of legal work is that it will, inevitably over time, lead to a continued shrinking in the scope of activities that constitutes legal work. Why? Because increasingly capable technology, together with an increasing array of talented non-legal professionals, will mean that a qualified lawyer does not necessarily need to do an ever-increasing range of work to the necessary standard.[161]

At one level this shrinking of the scope of traditional legal work will be viewed positively by in-house lawyers as one way to cope with increasing workloads. But at another level, all corporate lawyers will, understandably, worry about what work they will do in the future. That is precisely why the T-Shaped Lawyer vision, and the idea of doing business work, becomes so relevant and necessary.

C. Why business work matters more to you than legal work over time

Now that we have a clear idea of what constitutes legal work and the different types of business work, we can make some general observations about their relative importance to you over the course of your career.

At the beginning of your career as a lawyer, it is entirely appropriate to focus most of your time on developing your knowledge of the law, legal skills and doing legal work. After all, you want to become a legal expert as explained in Chapter 3.

However, for most corporate lawyers, over time, deepening that knowledge, honing those skills, and doing more and better legal work, is not as advantageous to your career prospects as developing business knowledge, business skills and being involved in both internal and client business work. The graphic below shows this view that is based on my personal experience and observations.

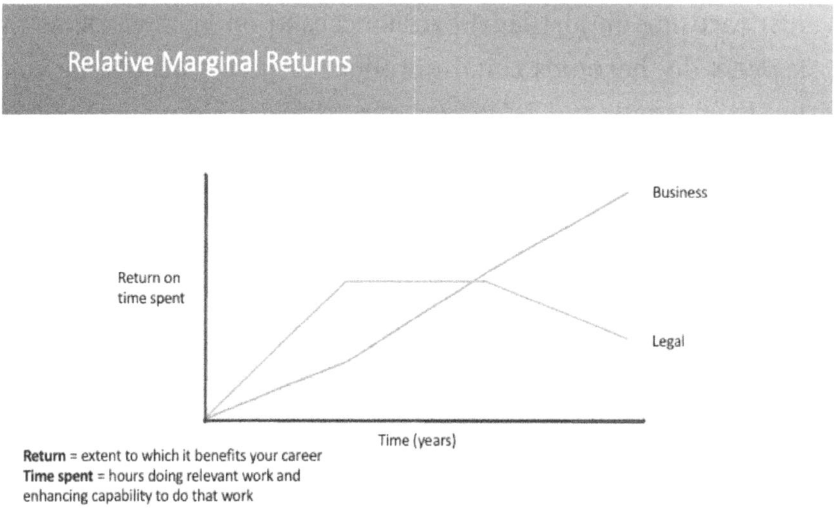

Just to be clear:

- The point in time when the balance tips in favour of a greater focus on business capabilities and business work varies depending on your role and whether you work in a legal department or firm. For those working in generalist roles in a legal department that tipping point comes much earlier in your career then if you work in an in-house specialist role or in a law firm.

- The return, on the investment of your time spent, is based on the extent to which the client business executives and the leaders of your legal department or firm generally value your legal work on the one hand compared with your business work on the other.

For most corporate lawyers, the marginal return on doing more, and getting better, at business work is greater than it is for legal work. Why? Because that is what clients and managers typically notice and value more especially as you progress in your career.

Just focusing on just legal excellence and on legal work, as most lawyers do, becomes counterproductive if you wish to be valued by your clients and to move into senior positions in your legal department or firm. But do not take my word for it. Ask those in senior positions in your department or firm whether it was legal work or business work that made the most significant difference in their career. Get more involved in internal business work and observe how those in senior positions respond. Do more client business work and notice the reaction from business executives to this work compared to their reaction to legal work.

The point of highlighting the relative marginal returns is that it is another data point to factor into the necessary exercise of regularly assessing what work you should, and should not, be doing.

D. <u>Work Rationalisation – how to change your current work</u>

Right at the beginning of the book, I stated that, in a world where most things are outside of your control, the two things that you have some control over are your work and your capabilities to do different work through your approach to professional development.

Understanding the different types of work that you can do as a lawyer and the relative merits of each is a great place to start, but **how can you change what work you do to do less of one type of work and more of another type of work?**

You might think that you have no control over your work because you must do what your client or manager wants you to do. In fact, both as individual lawyers and as a legal department or firm, you have a lot more opportunity to change your work than you think.

How can you change the work that you do and how you do it?

Most lawyers just focus on doing their work. Doing it as well and as efficiently as possible without giving too much thought to whether it is work that they should be doing at all or spending as much time as they do on it.

At risk of stating the obvious, if you want to change your work, you need to consciously think about the work that you do. You need to understand what work you are doing and how much time you spend on each category of work. Asking whether the work is legal work or not is a useful initial filter. Then, you need to assess this work using some specific criteria and decide whether, and if so how, you will make any one of several different possible changes. I refer to this crucial ongoing process as **work rationalisation** because it is about dispensing with certain types of work and about justifying changes to your work.

There are ways to change what work you do and how you do it, on your own and there are ways for legal departments and firms to do this at a team level.

As individuals

At the very least every lawyer can apply different priorities to different types of work. You can also allocate different amounts of time to different types of work. You may also be able to delegate work to others in your firm or company and/or outsource work to external providers.

If you believe there are opportunities to do one type of existing work in a different way, or to even eliminate this work, then you can propose that to the leaders in your firm or legal department.

Whatever changes you can make to your existing work, you can also look out for opportunities to support internal business work and initiate client business work. Business partnering, for example, is something anyone can do anytime in conjunction with your legal work without taking any additional time.

As a legal department

Individuals may be limited as to the extent to which they can change their work on their own. However, the leaders of legal departments have significant scope to change the existing work that lawyers do. Indeed, as I mentioned earlier in Chapter 7, it is the legal department, rather than the business executives, that establish the relevant legal processes in a company. That means that the leaders in legal departments have more scope than they typically believe to change existing work. As I said before, the only limitation tends to be your imagination, your risk appetite and the way things have always been done.

While most leaders have not taken full advantage of this opportunity to change, almost every legal department now routinely look for ways to do less of certain types of work typically through efficiency initiatives. The primary reason legal departments do this is so that lawyers can cope with their ever-increasing workloads. Whilst that is entirely appropriate and necessary, there must be other beneficial outcomes from undertaking this process. It must be more than just surviving and doing the same work more efficiently.

Many have suggested that one goal is *'to help us to do more complex and strategic legal work'*. But surely you are already doing this type of work and are not being prevented from doing so by other less important work?! A more compelling additional benefit of work rationalisation is so that you can do more business work of the type outlined in this book, especially client business work.

As a firm

Firms can also go through a similar work rationalisation process with a goal not so much of eliminating work but rather ascertaining the most cost-effective way to get that work done.

In summary, work rationalisation is a key process for individuals, legal departments, and firms to go through on a regular basis with the primary objective of:

- Identifying the following types of work to focus on:
    - legal work as defined.

    - client business work that adds value for clients.
    - supporting key internal business work.
- Finding ways to minimise or eliminate any other types of work.

CHAPTER 10

HOW TO TURN THE NEW VISION INTO REALITY

Now that we have clearly articulated 'the why' and defined 'the what', we are able to turn our attention to 'the how' to achieve this T- Shaped Lawyer vision.

Turning the new vision into reality requires a multi-faceted approach, as explained below. However, it is possible to summarise into four words, the essential change that most individuals, teams, and firms need to make:

'LESS LAW, MORE BUSINESS'

A. The 'Less Law More Business' Pivot

What I mean by this tagline is that to be a T-Shaped Lawyer most of you will need to make a change in three fundamental ways:

1. *Your Mindset*

   Think about yourself less as a lawyer and more as a businessperson.

   Does this mean you should not be proud that you are a lawyer? No.

   Does it mean forget that you are a lawyer or try to hide it? No.

   It means to think more of yourself as a businessperson, not just as a lawyer. That involves adopting a Businessperson Mindset and some of the suggestions in my second book.

2. *Your Work*

   Do less of your current work that you perceive to be legal work and do more business work.

   Does this mean doing your legal work at a lower standard? No.

   It means doing less of the work that you currently do that does not constitute legal work as defined in the prior chapter, and more business work as outlined in this book.

3. *Your Professional Development*

   Spend less time than you currently do developing your legal knowledge and skills, and more time than you currently do developing your business capabilities as detailed in my second book.

For some lawyers, this pivot will be a significant one. For others, who already think of themselves as a businessperson, do some business partnering and are involved in internal business work, they may only need to lean into the pivot a bit more.

But how can you make this pivot? How can you turn this T-Shaped Lawyer vision into reality for individuals, legal departments, or firms?

Just coming up with an ad hoc series of initiatives is not going to be sufficient. I frequently see lawyers, firms and legal departments randomly focusing on a few things like technology, design thinking or project management. This rarely results in any significant change in the capabilities of the lawyers or in the work they do.

Why you need a Framework

To avoid this trap, and because there are many key components to achieve a vision, you need a framework. A framework is a comprehensive 'scaffolding' specifically designed to help you formulate strategies to achieve a desired outcome. If you use the scaffolding to rebuild your new self or your new legal department or firm, then you are more likely to achieve that outcome.

Another way to think about a framework is that it is an attempt to make sense of a complex mix of otherwise confusing things. In the absence of a framework, you are basically making random guesses about what to focus on in individual professional development, or in legal department or firm strategy. Of course, a framework is only as good as those who designed them, and the purpose for which the framework was designed.

In recent years, there have been a few frameworks developed for lawyers that focus beyond the law and legal skills.

Examples:

- The Delta Model[162], developed by a group of US academics, offers a comprehensive and useful framework for lawyers and non-legal professionals without steering them in any direction. It covers individual competency development.
- The O-Shaped Lawyer Framework[163] has gained some traction in the UK. Its mantra is 'people first' and it has the highly laudable goal of encouraging the formation and development of rounded lawyers in a diverse, inclusive, and healthier environment.

However, the primary focus of these frameworks, which are only for use in the legal profession, is not on how lawyers can add more value; they do not offer one vision that can be applied with frameworks at the individual lawyer, legal department, and firm level to truly transform the type of work done in the corporate legal industry and the impact on clients; and they are not designed to achieve the T-Shaped Lawyer vision.

To achieve that vision, the framework needs to be specifically designed for that purpose. The framework can then be used to develop transformation plans at an individual lawyer, legal department, and firm level.

The T-Shaped frameworks below are based on my own personal experience as a lawyer, and later as a consultant, over many decades. They have been tried, tested, and refined with lawyers, legal departments, and firms world-wide since 2015. They provide a comprehensive step-by-step structure, and they are aligned with each other to facilitate the adoption of the T-Shaped Lawyer or Legal Expert Business Generalist vision, across the entire corporate legal industry.

B. Individual Lawyers: The T-Shaped Lawyer Framework™

For individuals to turn the T-Shaped Lawyer vision into reality involves, over time, changing your work and yourself.

Changes to Your Work

The change required to your work is outlined in detail in this book. In general, for those new to this work, the change starts with business partnering more frequently and looking for business leadership and internal business work opportunities as and when these arise. For those who may already be doing some business work, it generally involves leaning into it more over time and helping others to do it more often.

It is important to understand that the T-Shaped Lawyer is not an 'all-or-nothing' vision as shown in the Spectrum below.

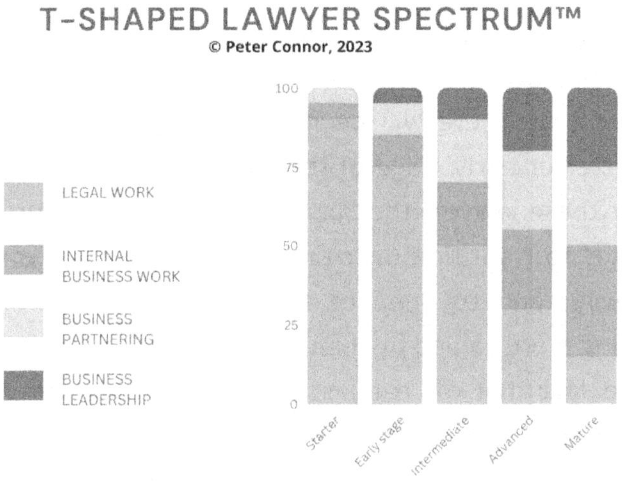

There are a few points to highlight about this Spectrum:

- The percentages of relative time spent doing the different types of work are not intended to be precise. Rather they are intended to give a general, and very approximate, indication of the extent to which anyone is a T-Shaped Lawyer.

- The spectrum maps quite closely with the typical career path of an in-house lawyer. For example, junior lawyers typically start doing mostly legal work[164] and perhaps 'dipping their toes' in the business partnering and internal business work waters. As lawyers become more experienced, they typically increase the amount of client business work and get more involved in doing or supporting internal business work including managing and developing other lawyers. Most general counsels spend very little time doing legal work and almost all their time doing a range of different types of business work.
- That said, there will be many senior lawyers who are at a starter or early stage of the evolution to a T-Shaped Lawyer. For these lawyers the Spectrum provides a picture of what it takes to transition over time to become more of a T-Shaped Lawyer and to enhance their prospects of promotion and being more valued by their clients.
- The fact that, at early stages of the Spectrum, lawyers do relatively little business work does not mean that it is not important at that stage. On the contrary, business work is typically noticed and valued more than legal work by clients and superiors in the firm and legal department. Also, if you wish to move into a senior role in a firm or a legal department, then you need to do more business work over time and not wait until you are ready for such a role.
- Not everyone will attain the vision and become a mature T-Shaped Lawyer and that is perfectly fine. Attaining that status is the aspirational goal but even just moving along the Spectrum over time will reap many of the benefits outlined in the book.

- The Spectrum also broadly applies to lawyers working in firms with the mature stage approximating the work of a managing partner. That said, there will typically be slightly less business partnering and slightly more legal work at all stages for such lawyers.
- You can, and I do, adopt a similar approach, using the T-Shaped Lawyer Framework, to assess anyone's capability to do the different types of work.

Moving along the Spectrum to realise the T-Shaped Lawyer vision, involves not just doing more business work, it involves developing new knowledge and capabilities to do this work.

Changes to Yourself

Up until now, your professional development probably consisted of keeping up to date on the law, attending the odd webinar or conference, and doing the odd course on random topics such as leadership, coding, legal design and doing more effective presentations.

Changing your vision as an individual changes your professional development needs which in turn changes you and your professional capabilities.

Now, if you are serious about becoming a T-Shaped Lawyer, then it is important to change yourself and your capabilities in a very specific way. For that you need a more structured and focused approach to your professional development - one that is designed to achieve that objective.

The T-Shaped Lawyer Framework, as shown below in a generic version, is designed specifically to help individuals become T-

Shaped Lawyers and to do not just legal work but also business work, especially client business work.

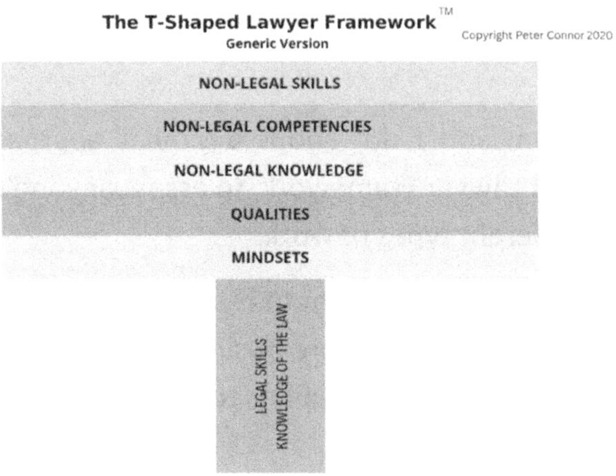

This detailed version of the Framework and how to use it, together with a personal framework, as the basis for your professional development is explained in detail in my second book – *The T-Shaped Lawyer Guidebook: A Framework for Your Professional Development*.

B. Legal Ops and Other Legal Professionals

I am often asked whether the T-Shaped vision can apply to professionals who are not lawyers and work in legal departments or firms in areas like legal operations, technology, or business development.

One of the many attractions of the T-Shaped Lawyer vision and Framework is that it can be adapted to apply to any professional working in a legal department or firm because it is based on the T-Shaped professional concept that has been applied to virtually every type of professional and profession.

How can such professionals adopt the T-Shaped model and adapt the T-Shaped Lawyer vision? Obviously, your primary area of expertise and work – your vertical axis – will not be legal work and legal advice. Rather it will be legal operations or whatever your primary role is in the legal department or firm. Typically, this will involve one form or another of internal business work.

However, on the horizontal axis, you can also support client business work. Helping to design, build, purchase and support systems and processes to enable business and functional executives to obtain the legal information and documents they need, would be one example of client business work. Plus you can help educate the lawyers on some of the skills required to do client business work so that they can at least identify client business work opportunities.

With one or two minor tweaks, the T-Shaped Lawyer Framework depicted above can be used as the basis for your professional development, to help you to be a T-Shaped professional.

C. Legal Departments: The T-Shaped Team Framework™

Since writing the first version of this book, many leaders of legal departments have told me that the T-Shaped Lawyer vision puts into words something they relate to, because they do think of themselves as a businessperson, and they do client business work as well as internal business work. That is encouraging and not that surprising because it is difficult to be in a senior leadership position without being a T-Shaped Lawyer. However, almost all these leaders have not thought much about this topic and not spoken to their legal colleagues or clients about it.

If you are a leader in a legal department and you understand the importance of being a T-Shaped Lawyer, then you have an opportunity, if not a responsibility, to spread the word in your legal department and in the corporate legal industry. It is time to shine a light on this dark art and now, with this book, you have the terminology and explanations to use for that purpose.

As a leader in a legal department, you can turn the T-Shaped Lawyer vision into reality at three different levels:

Level 1

Speaking about it with your legal colleagues is the starting point for how you can turn this vision into reality for your legal department. You can also discuss it with your peers from other organisations. I highly recommend that you use the book itself, or the least the terminology in the book, as I have seen some well-intentioned lawyers confuse the message by trying to put the key points in their own words or confusing 'the what' with 'the how'.

Level 2

The next thing you can do as a leader is to help individual lawyers in your legal department become T-Shaped Lawyers. Remember that you can do that in two ways:

- helping to change their work to do more business work.
- and helping to change their capability to do new work.

You can help your colleagues to change their work immediately through a combination of a work rationalisation process and encouraging them to at least engage in business partnering and understand internal business work.

When it comes to enhancing the capabilities of those in your department you have a few different options. **One 'hands off 'approach** is to simply provide them all with a copy of the second book and provide time and financial support for them to use The T-Shaped Lawyer Framework as the basis for their professional development on their own.

If you are serious about enhancing the capabilities of the legal team for internal and client business work, it is essential to revisit and, typically overhaul, the legal department's approach to professional development.

Another option is to adopt **a more 'hands on' approach,** as some[165] are choosing to do, you can use the Framework as the basis for training and development programs for the entire legal department as explained in the second book.

Level 3

The more you think about the T-Shaped Lawyer vision, the more you will realise that turning it into reality extends way beyond professional development. It changes literally everything as depicted in the graphic below of the T-Shaped Team Framework™.

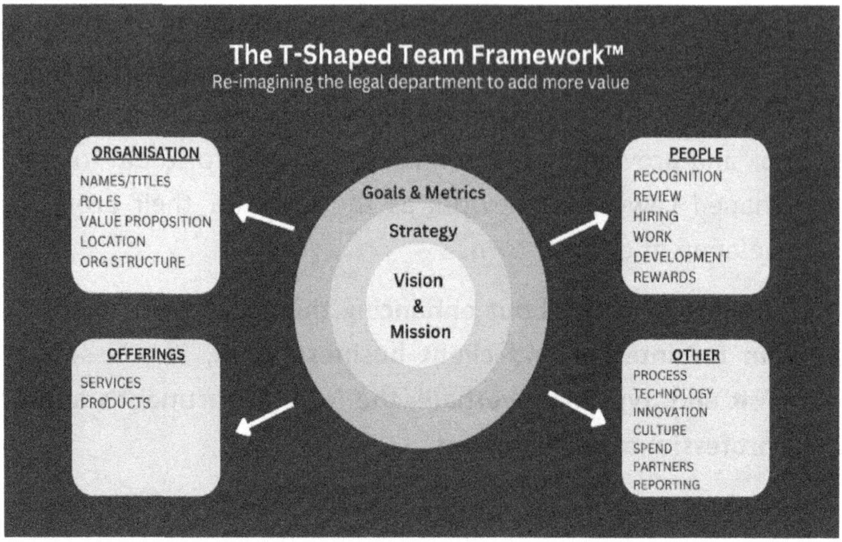

A detailed explanation of this Framework is beyond the scope of this book. However, it should be evident to leaders that adopting this new vision at a team level allows you to reframe the conventional change perspective of trying to deliver legal services more efficiently. It allows you to truly reimagine all aspects of a legal department and to transform, not just improve, it so that it delivers more value for the organisation and prepares your team for the future.

E. Law Firms: The T-Shaped Firm Framework™

Adopting the new vision for a law firm changes everything just as it does for a legal department. Again, explaining this is beyond the scope of this book. However, the above Framework for legal departments provides an indication of how firms can transform themselves along similar lines but with important differences to reflect the different perspective and position of a firm.

CONCLUSION

The landscape for all lawyers and other professionals working in corporate legal departments and corporate law firms is constantly changing. The pace, magnitude and even the nature of change is different now. Some are talking about, and in some cases initiating, change in legal departments and in firms but it is mostly to internal processes and systems. Lawyers and other are impacted by these changes but there have been no material changes to the types of work that lawyers do and to their capabilities to do new types of work. In other words, there may have been a degree of process and digital transformation but no human transformation.

The question for all corporate lawyers to consider is ***'do you need to change yourself and your work more than you are currently doing?'***

The answer to that question depends on whether you believe that aspiring to be a better lawyer, and to deliver better quality legal services more efficiently, is sufficient now and into the future. If you believe that then you have answered the question in the negative. However, if you are not sure, or you agree with the arguments in this book that this default vision will be insufficient, then you need a new vision. You need a vision that captures what you do aspire to become and what changes you need to make to achieve it.

As an individual lawyer, and as a legal department and firm, it is imperative to first clarify what you are trying to achieve by making any changes. While you may have many different reasons to change, I have suggested that your paramount objective of change should be to **add more value** especially for your clients.

Why?

Adding more value addresses many of the typical reasons for change and is the one higher order objective that is shared by individuals, legal departments, firms, and clients. It also happens to be crucial to work rationalisation, innovation and aligns with prevailing views about the future of work.

The way to add more value, especially for clients, is not just by focusing on the quality or efficiency of legal service delivery or improving to be a better lawyer. These are the prevailing paradigms in the corporate legal industry. Rather, it requires a new direction, one that focuses on transforming individual lawyers, not just systems and processes, to be different and to develop different capabilities to do different more effective work.

This new vision involves you aspiring to become a businessperson, not just a lawyer, who provides business input and advice, not just legal advice, and does business work, not just legal work, for the benefit of businesses, not just the legal department or firm.

I have proposed the T-Shaped Lawyer, a form of legal expert business generalist, to represent this new vision for reasons outlined in the book. A simplified high-level description of the new vision is shown in the graphic below.

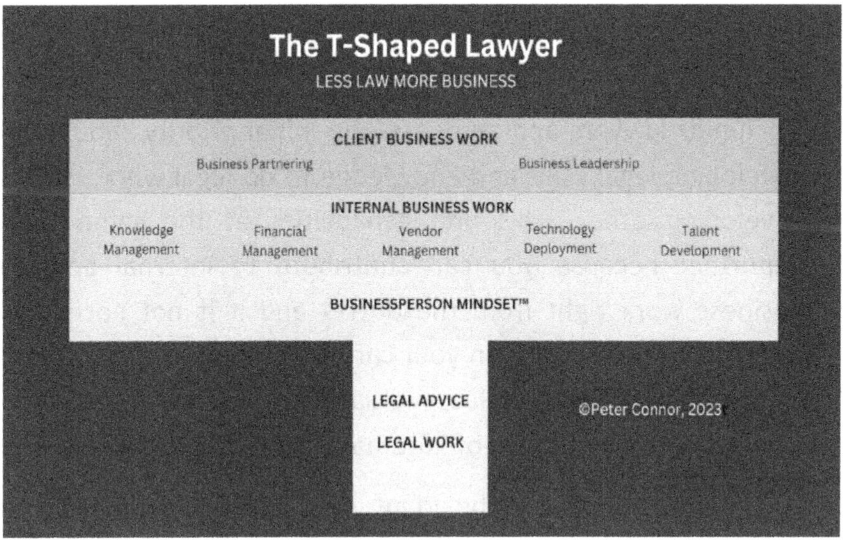

This vision can be adopted by every corporate lawyer, at any stage of your career, and adapted to your unique circumstances.

Internal business work is part of the vision, not because most lawyers need to do much of this work but because you need to understand and support this work which is increasingly done by others. As important at internal business work is for legal departments and firms, it is client business work that is the most important aspect of this new vision. Why? Because internal business work primarily benefits the legal department or firm. Client business work is the most effective way to add more value for the benefit of clients.

Client business work is more accessible for in-house lawyers especially those in generalist roles. However, even those in specialist roles and law firm lawyers can also incorporate business partnering into their advice work, identify business leadership opportunities, and support legal departments with internal business work.

For junior lawyers and students, the initial priority should be on developing legal skills and knowledge to do legal work. However, developing other skills and capabilities at the same time is important because you can contribute to internal and client business work right from the outset and it is not necessary to transform yourself later in your career. It might also be important in case it is difficult, at least initially, for you to find traditional legal work to do because of automation of entry level legal work.

The new vision can even be adapted by legal operations and other professionals who are not lawyers because it is based on the T-Shaped professional construct that has been applied to almost every type of professional.

The rewards for adopting this new vision are significant and include future proofing yourself as much as possible; becoming a true trusted advisor to, and being more valued by, key clients; and thriving and maximising your professional fulfilment, performance, and success.

The more your career progresses, the more important business work, and the capabilities to do that work, becomes as shown by the T-Shaped Lawyer Spectrum™ and the increasing marginal returns from business work as mentioned earlier.

Finally, the vision can be adopted and applied at a legal department and firm level, not just an individual lawyer level. The vision offers a new direction for all and a way to reframe the current conventional approach to change in the corporate legal industry. It literally changes everything.

For individuals, how to turn the vision into reality, through a different approach to your professional development, is explained in detail in the second book on the T-Shaped Lawyer Framework™. Turning the vision into reality for legal departments is covered in the T-Shaped Team Framework™ and, for firms, in the T-Shaped Firm Framework™.

My aim in writing this book is to challenge the conventional idea of what it means to be a corporate lawyer and to reframe the name of the game for legal departments and firms beyond the efficient delivery of legal services. I hope it provides you with the guidance and inspiration to pursue this new direction that will enhance the impact of your work and better prepare you for whatever may happen in the future.

I want to acknowledge some people who have provided me with wonderful opportunities and support over the years to discover this new way of working as a lawyer. I would like to specifically call out Geoff Taperell, David Shannon, and Ray Black during our time together at Baker McKenzie; Stephen Clayton, Rod Steedman, John Croll, and Brian Martin during our time together at Sun Microsystems; and David Friedman and Tony Gomes during our time together at Citrix Systems: and Santhi Latha at the Rajah & Tann Asia Academy. Last, but by no means least, my wife, Penny, who bore the brunt of endless geographic moves to support my career and endless talk about writing these books.

ABOUT THE AUTHOR

Peter Connor is the Founder & CEO of AlternativelyLegal which he formed in 2015 to help corporate lawyers, in-house legal departments and law firms innovate and transform – not just improve – the way they work. He does that through a range of unique programs and frameworks that he has delivers in workshops or consulting engagements including:

- **T-shaped Lawyer Program™** designed for legal departments and firms to provide guidance and inspiration to individual lawyers on the T-Shaped Lawyer Framework™ and how to utilise it to enhance their capabilities to become T-Shaped Lawyers so that they can do more meaningful and impactful business work, not just legal work.
- **T-shaped Team Program™** designed to provide guidance to legal departments on the T-Shaped Team Framework™ and how to utilise it to transform the legal department into a team that provides not only legal services, but also business services and products.
- **T-shaped Firm Program™** designed to provide guidance to law firms on The T-Shaped Firm Framework™ and how to utilise it to transform the firm into a business that provides a range of business services and products not just legal services.

Peter has conducted over 50 workshops around the world for the legal departments of a range of brand name companies including Google, HSBC, Pfizer, ANT Financial / Alibaba, Porsche, Coca Cola, Bayer, AIA, and ANZ Bank. He has also worked with firms like Baker McKenzie, Minter Ellison, and Rajah & Tann Asia.

In Australia, Peter was retained by KPMG Law to help them conceive, develop, and deliver their New Law / Legal Operations and Transformation Services product and service offerings for in-house legal departments.

Prior to starting AlternativelyLegal, he worked in a business role, as VP Tech Products, managing software development for the Hong Kong-based compliance firm, Red Flag Group.

Peter has had a diverse, global career as a lawyer for over 25 years. He has lived and worked in Silicon Valley California, Switzerland, England, Hong Kong, and Sydney in the following roles:

- European General Counsel and, later, as Head of Global Compliance for Citrix Systems
- APAC General Counsel, Head of Legal Shared Services, European General Counsel and Head of European Government Affairs for Sun Microsystems.
- Senior Associate at Baker McKenzie in Sydney and Hong Kong.

Peter is the recipient of the Citrix Design Thinking Hero Award and the Sun Microsystems CEO Business Leadership Award for his innovative contributions to the business. He is a widely- published author and Legal Business World, and others, have recognised him as a global thought leader. He regularly speaks at legal conferences around the world on innovation and transformation. He can be contacted at peter.connor@alternativelylegal.com or by connecting on LinkedIn.

ENDNOTES

[1] I don't like to use the expression 'client' to describe the business and functional work colleagues of an in-house lawyer. However, I will use this expression in this book to avoid confusion for those who only use that expression.

[2] The use of the word 'soft' implies that they are of lesser importance to 'hard' skills or that they are optional. Nothing could be further fromthe truth.

[3] Legal Business World, 2023 https://peterconnor.legalbusinesslibrary.com/

[4] The most important key points will be highlighted in bold text.

[5] *The Fourth Industrial Revolution*, Klaus Schwab, Crown, 15 January 2017

[6] *21 Lessons for the 21st Century:* Yuval Harari, Speigel & Grau and Jonathan Cape August 2018

[7] *An Everyone Culture: Becoming a Deliberately Developmental Organization*, Lisa Lahey and Robert Kegan. Harvard Business Review Press (22 March 2016)

[8] Ditto

[9] Ditto

[10] Marc Andressen, *Why Software is Eating the World*, The Wall Street Journal, August 20,2011

[11] Open AI's ChatGPT is the latest example of what technology is capable of. It was only released a few months prior to writing this book, so it is too early to tell. However, early indications are that even the current version may be capable of doing many things that lawyers currently do - including research, contract drafting and even basic negotiation, to a good enough standard especially if checked by a lawyer.

[12] See for example *Legal Upheaval*: Michelle Stefano at page 22-26

[13] *The Future of the Professions*: Richard Susskind and Daniel Susskind, OUP Oxford 2015

[14] Richard Susskind describes these new jobs in the latest version of his book *Tomorrow's Lawyers,* Oxford University Press, 2023. I comment on this later in my book.

[15] For a description of Agile At Scale see for example https://hbr.org/2018/05/agile-at-scale

[16] Lynda Gratton and Andrew Scott, *The 100-year life: Living and Working in an age of longevity*, Bloomsbury, 1st Edition June 2, 2016. see also http://www.100yearlife.com/

[17] *The Adaptation Advantage*, Heather McGowan and Chris Shipley, Wiley 1st Edition March 27, 2020

[18] *An Everyone Culture: Becoming a Deliberately Developmental Organization*, Lisa Lahey and Robert Kegan. Harvard Business Review Press (22 March 2016)
[19] https://www.oecd.org/employment/future-of-work/
[20] https://ec.europa.eu/social/main.jsp?catId=88&eventsId=1386&furtherEvents=yes&langId=en
[21] https://www.weforum.org/reports/the-future-of-jobs-report-2018
[22] *The Adaptation Advantage*, Heather McGowan and Chris Shipley, Wiley 1st Edition March 27, 2020 at P12
[23] https://www.pwc.com/gx/en/services/people-organisation/workforce-of-the-future/workforce-of-the-future-the-competing-forces-shaping-2030-pwc.pdf Quote from Carol Stubbings, Global Leader People and Organisations PWC.
[24] https://iaals.du.edu/publications/foundations-practice-whole-lawyer-and-character-quotient
[25] https://www.lawdeltamodel.com/
[26] https://oshaped.com/
[27] While there are increasingly firms and other legal service providers that are trying to move away from some of these generalisations, they are apt for the vast majority of lawyers working in firms worldwide.
[28] *Getting In and Out of the House: The Worlds of In-House Counsel, Big Law, and the Emerging Career Trajectories of In-House Lawyers*. Eli Wald. Fordham Law Review Volume 88 Issue 5 Article 10, 2020 . See also Carl D. Liggio, Sr., *A Look at the Role of Corporate Counsel: Back to the Future— or Is It the Past?* 44 ARIZ. L. REV. 621, 621 (2002).
[29] See for example https://www.swaab.com.au/assets/download/LPRU-Wellbeing-report-2021.pdf and https://lsbc.vic.gov.au/lawyers/practising-law/lawyer-wellbeing/wellbeing-resources/why-poor-wellbeing-so-common-law
[30] See for example, https://lawyerwellbeing.net/, https://www.lawsociety.com.au/resources/mental-health-and-wellbeing, https://mail.google.com/mail/u/1/#search/The+resilient/KtbxLxGgFSvfvRhTQFsSqpHvSBrjbgqffL?projector=1&messagePartId=0.1 and https://mail.google.com/mail/u/1/#search/The+resilient/KtbxLxGgFSvfvRhTQFsSqpHvSBrjbgqffL?projector=1&messagePartId=0.2
[31] Jordan Furlong https://www.law21.ca/2019/09/the-new-legal-economy/ See also *The Great Legal Reformation*: Mitch Kowalski, iUniverse September 2017
[32] See for example *Law is a Buyer's Market*: Jordan Furlong, Kindle Edition. A buyer's market, for those who are not familiar with the expression, implies that

buyers now can dictate terms more, or at least have more influence over those terms, and, as a result, drive change if they want to. Whether in-house lawyers are driving change as much as they could is a matter of debate.

[33] One of the first to point this out was Mark Harris the founder of Axiom Law. He said *"The incumbent model is largely artisanal. It's perfect for novel challenges that are irreducibly complex, but it's not necessary for the bulk of commerce."* https://www.forbes.com/sites/danielfisher/2015/02/12/legal-services-firms-73-million-deal-strips-the-mystery-from-derivatives-trading/#5e46112fcca7

[34] Strictly speaking the client is the corporation but in practise it is typically the in-house lawyer, if there is one, who initiates the buying of services or products.

[35] https://www.acc.com/

[36] https://ecla.online/

[37] https://in-housecounselworldwide.com/

[38] *Tomorrow's Lawyers*, Richard Susskind. Oxford University Press UK, 3rd Edition May 2,2023

[39] One typical problem is this 'extracurricular' work is often not the right kind of non-legal work. This book highlights what is the right kind of non-legal work for lawyers.

[40] See for example *The Generalist Counsel: How Leading General Counsel Are Shaping Tomorrow's Companies*. Prashant Dubey and Eva Kripalani Oxford University Press 2013. *Indispensable Counsel: The Chief Legal Officer In The New Reality*: E. Norman Veasey, Christine T. Di Guglielmo. Oxford University Press 2013. *The Inside Counsel Revolution: Resolving the Partner-Guardian Tension.* Benjamin W Heineman Jr. American Bar Association 2016

[41] The expression unbundling of work was coined by Richard Susskind in his book *The End of Lawyers? Rethinking the Nature of Legal Services:* Oxford University Press, 2010

[42] https://www.buyinglegal.com/

[43] https://legaloperators.com/, https://legalops.com/, https://www.legalopsuncensored.com/, https://linkforlegal.com/

[44] https://cloc.org/what-is-legal-operations/ provides a more detailed explanation of each core area of legal operations.

[45] https://www.acc.com/maturity

[46] See for example, https://www.bcg.com/en-us/publications/2018/how-diverse-leadership-teams-boost-innovation.aspx and https://legal.thomsonreuters.com/en/insights/articles/law-diversity-inclusion

[47] https://www.diversitylab.com/pilot-projects/mansfield-rule-legal-department-edition/

[48] For example, Slack, Microsoft Teams and Office 365, Zoom, Google Docs and Meet.

[49] Example of this is Microsoft Legal's development of a tool called HiveMind that uses tagging to automatically store and retrieve email legal advice provided by the legal department and by their external advisors.

[50] For example, Kanban or visual to-do boards see for example https://files.clio.com/marketo/ebooks/lean-legal-three-techniques-for-the-agile-lawyer.pdf

[51] Co-creation is a special kind of collaboration that involves working with a customer to develop solutions for them.

[52] Hackathons are events involving a diverse mix of individuals who attempt in a compressed period of time to solve problems typically involving the development of technology solutions.

[53] Personal branding involves defining and promoting what you stand for to differentiate yourself. Consultants are available to help you to enhance your personal branding.

[54] See for example InView created by LawVu, The General Counsel Forum created by Exigent, Legal Ninjas and Crafty Counsel

[55] https://docket.acc.com/t-shaped-lawyer-language-change-and-importance-precision

[56] Such as IBM Watson, Microsoft Power Apps, Neota Logic, Checkbox and Josef

[57] For example, Walters Kluwer, Mitratech, Thomson Reuters and Onit

[58] For example, Plexus Gateway, LawVu, Xakia

[59] http://www3.weforum.org/docs/WEF_Towards_a_Reskilling_Revolution.pdf. at page 23

[60] George Beaton is the founder of Beaton Consulting and, in conjunction with Imme Kaschner, he wrote the book *'Remaking Law Firms: Why and How'*: American Bar Association, June 7, 2016.

[61] For example, Allen&Overy Peerpoint, Pinsent Masons Vario, Corrs Orbit and Minters Flex.

[62] For example, DLA Piper partnering with Exari to offer Documents As A Service, Norton Rose Fulbright Deal Vault, Contractor Check and Parker.

[63] Allen&Overy Fuse

[64] For example, Dentons' investment in Nextlaw Labs/Ross Technology, Minter Ellison acquiring a technology consulting business IT Newcom

[65] https://www.thomsonreuters.com/en-us/posts/legal/alsp-report-2023/

[66] For example, Advent Balance/Lawyers on Demand
[67] For example, Morae/Exigent
[68] For example, Plexus and LawVu
[69] For example, Major Lindsey and Africa MLA Global started as a recruitment business and now also offers interim lawyers and consulting to legal departments and law firms.
[70] For example, EY acquired the non-technology part of Riverview Law and it acquired the Pangea3 managed services business which Thomson Reuters had acquired a few years earlier. Also, Elevate has acquired Yerra Solutions, Halebury, Lex Predict and Cognatio Law. LOD merged with Advent Balance and acquired Lexvoco.
[71] By Michael Huber and by Eric Chin, formerly of Beaton Consulting.
[72] Ibid endnote 63
[73] https://techindex.law.stanford.edu/
[74] Legal Zoom is the pioneer in this space enabling individuals and small businesses to help themselves by making legal documents and easy access to affordable back up advisory services. There are now many similar businesses throughout the world.
[75] For example, Walters Kluwer, Mitratech, Thomson Reuters and Onit
[76] For example, Plexus Gateway, LawVu, Xakia
[77] https://fintechcircle.com/legaltech-book/, *The Legal Tech Ecosystem,* Colin Levy, Ramses House Publishing, 2023, *The Legal Innovation Handbook*, Nicola Shaver, Global Law& Business, 30 November 2022,
[78] https://legaltechnology.com/, https://www.lawsitesblog.com/
https://www.artificiallawyer.com/, https://www.legalitprofessionals.com/, https://legaltechtrends.substack.com/, https://www.legaltechnologyhub.com/
[79] such as European Legal Technology Association (ELTA), Australian Legal Technology Association (ALTA) and the International Legal Technology Association (ILTA).
[80] https://www.globallegaltechreport.com/
[81] Ibid endnote 17 at P2
[82] *The Age of Unreason*: Charles Handy, Harvard Business Review Press; 1st edition (February 1, 1991)
[83] Christensen & Bower, 1996; Tushman, Smith, Wood, Westerman, & O'Reilly, 2003 in Gilbert, 2005) referred to in https://managingresearchlibrary.org/glossary/discontinuous-change
[84] See for example Richard Susskind who states '*I forsee discontinuity over time and the emergence of a legal industry that will be quite alien to the current legal establishment*' in the introduction to *Tomorrow's Lawyers,*

Oxford University Press , 3rd edition, 2023.
[85] Ibid endnote 82 at Page 5
[86] Ibid endnote 82 at Page 19
[87] https://www.thebritishacademy.ac.uk/publishing/review/34/british-academy-review-34-ai-work-and-outcome-thinking/
[88] Ibid endnote 14
[89] See for example https://www.qls.com.au/getattachment/c198ec41-5b0b-4702-b236-625231d3b772/booklet-the-resilient-lawyer.pdf
[90] In recognition of the crucial role that personal factors play in professional success and fulfilment, these factors are explicitly featured in the T-Shaped Lawyer Framework as explained in my second book.
[91] General counsel may, from time to time, have other specific priorities. However, the one crucial priority that applies always is adding more value.
[92] Presentation to GC 100 Chapter of ACC in Australia reported in the Australian Financial Review on December 14 ,2022, at page 6.
[93] My book is about changing what lawyers do to add more value. There is an excellent book by Sterling Miller which is primarily about how to market the value that in-house lawyers provide from existing work. I commend it to you because there are some terrific ideas in it for how to market not only what you currently do but the value you add by doing new work. See https://www.amazon.com.au/Showing-Value-Legal-Department-Center/dp/1639050450
[94] https://www2.deloitte.com/us/en/insights/focus/technology-and-the-future-of-work/what-is-work.html
[95] https://www2.deloitte.com/us/en/insights/focus/technology-and-the-future-of-work/redefining-work-for-new-value-creation.html
[96] See for example https://www.atlassian.com/blog/productivity/the-problem-with-productivity-metrics
[97]
https://www.ted.com/talks/dan_gilbert_the_psychology_of_your_future_self?language=en
[98] Ibid endnote 97
[99] Refer to the T-Shaped Team Framework™ shown in the final chapter of the book.
[100] https://clp.law.harvard.edu/assets/educating-the-digital-lawyer.pdf and https://www.ft.com/reports/digital-lawyers
[101] Richard G. Shell of the Wharton School at the University of Pennsylvania https://www.abajournal.com/magazine/article/the_strategic_lawyer1) and later Sterling Miller https://sterlingmiller2014.wordpress.com/2019/12/12/ten-things-the-strategic-in-house-lawyer/

[102] https://iaals.du.edu/publications/foundations-practice-whole-lawyer-and-character-quotient
[103] https://thefluidlawyer.legalbusinesslibrary.com/index-h5.html?page=1#page=1
[104] Ibid endnote 26
[105] https://corpgov.law.harvard.edu/2010/09/05/the-general-counsel-as-lawyer-statesman/ See also for general counsel - https://books.google.com.au/books/about/The_Generalist_Counsel.html?id=DUguAAAAQBAJ&redir_esc=y
[106] Ibid endnote 14
[107] *Getting In and Out of the House: The Worlds of In-House Counsel, Big Law, and the Emerging Career Trajectories of In-House Lawyers*. Eli Wald. Fordham Law Review Volume 88 Issue 5 Article 10, 2020 quoting from Carl D. Liggio, Sr., *A Look at the Role of Corporate Counsel: Back to the Future—or Is It the Past?*, 44 ARIZ. L. REV. 621, 621 (2002).
[108] See for example *The Generalist Counsel*. Prashant Dubey and Eva Kripalani. Oxford University Press, 1st Edition (August 27, 2013)
[109] These include interpersonal skills and leadership capabilities as outlined in my second book.
[110] See for example https://www.forbes.com/sites/markcohen1/2021/12/16/legal-transformation-is-a-business-story/?sh=3bb3a1aa58a1 and Catherine McGregor's - *Business Thinking in Practise for In-house Counsel* - https://www.globelawandbusiness.com/books/Business-Thinking-in-Practice-for-In-House-Counsel
[111] https://www.forbes.com/sites/michaelsimmons/2015/03/23/how-one-life-hack-from-a-self-made-billionaire-leads-to-exceptional-success/?sh=4d9561c2543d
[112] Ibid endnote 17 at page 12.
[113] https://www.talentgrow.com/blog/should-you-be-expert-generalist
[114] See for example Joe Longo the chairman of Australia's corporate regulator, ASIC, saying that lawyers may face legal charges if they fail to intervene, when they should, in business discussions. He said "It's not just about the law. A good general counsel will help boards and companies make good decisions about what transactions to enter into, who to do business with and manage reputational risks." Presentation to GC 100 Chapter of ACC in Australia reported in the Australian Financial Review on December 14 at page 6.
[115] This point about marginal benefits is shown graphically in Chapter 9
[116] 'Succeeding through Service Innovation' - http://www.ceri.msu.edu/wp-content/uploads/2010/06/Cambridge_T-Shaped.pdf

[117] Cotter, P. (2015). *Hiring and development, down to a T. Chief Learning Officer, 14*(2) and Harris, P. (2009). *Help wanted: "T-shaped" skills to meet 21st century needs. T+D, 63*(9)
[118] See David Guest, *"The hunt is on for the Renaissance Man of computing,"* The Independent, September 17, 1991.The concept was popularized by Tim Brown, the CEO of Ideo, when referring to the type of person his famous design studio seeks to recruit.
[119] HR - https://www.aihr.com/blog/why-t-shaped-hr/, Sales - https://www.saleslabs.io/t-shaped-sales-development-program/, Marketing - https://buffer.com/resources/t-shaped-marketer/ , Finance - https://corporatefinanceinstitute.com/resources/management/t-shaped-skills/ ,Business Analyst - https://masteringbusinessanalysis.com/mba050-the-t-shaped-business-analyst/, Product Manager - https://medium.com/hackernoon/the-t-shaped-product-manager-2019-part-1-core-competencies-c1c65456c4d9, DevOps - https://www.exin.com/article/devops-the-next-generation-3-ways-t-shaped-skills-are-important-in-devops-teams/, Engineers - https://www.researchgate.net/figure/T-shaped-professional-engineers-and-t-shaped-engineering-technologists_fig1_256755322, Software developers - https://www.opencirclesolutions.nl/t-shaped-open-source-software-developers/,
[120] *New Directions for Adult and Continuing Education,* 2016 Wiley Periodicals Inc. Chapter 5: Navigating Professional White Water: Rethinking Continuing Professional Education at Work. Professor Laura Bierema, Professor and Associate Dean for Academic Programs at the University of Georgia, USA.
[121] https://dashboard.mazsystems.com/webreader/31892?page=34
[122] https://docket.acc.com/t-shaped-lawyer
[123] https://www.legalbusinessworld.com/post/2017/12/22/the-t-shaped-lawyer
[124] This simplified visual has been significantly refined and enhanced as I intend to show in *the T-Shaped Lawyer Guidebook* my second book.
[125] See for example https://www.acc.com/resource-library/if-other-hat-fits-wear-it-guide-effective-business-partnering
[126] Your non-legal work will initially be less frequent than your legal work although, over time, this may change if you believe in the redefining work idea proposed by Deloitte Insight experts mentioned earlier in the book.
[127] As I mention in several places in the book, people lack precision about the language they use to describe change. The reason I have claimed this expression as a trademark is simply because I do not want others to misuse this

expression to describe something else such as being business minded. Everyone is free to use the Businessperson Mindset. I only ask that it be used only as defined in this book.

[128] Dr. Jacob Towery, adjunct clinical instructor in the department of psychiatry at Stanford University

[129] Ibid endnote 17

[130] One exception would be charity, social or pro-bono work.

[131] See Chapter 9

[132] See for example the name of the LegalOps.com conference in October 2023 is *Running Legal Like a Business.*

[133] There are various reasons to explain why the lawyers who do work in this way don't talk about it. One of those reasons is because, until this book, no-one has spelled it out clearly and provided a set of defined terms for everyone to use.

[134] There are many other explanations including the fact that there is a huge, and ever-growing, ecosystem of stakeholders that have a vested interest in the continued focus on internal business work. They have lots to lose, and little to gain, if the primary focus switches to client business work.

[135] Many firms often tout their internal business work as of benefit to clients but in reality, more often than not, the primary beneficiary is the firm and the benefit to in-house or business clients is marginal.

[136] See for example https://www.globelawandbusiness.com/books/business-development-a-practical-handbook-for-lawyers-second-edition, https://www.sage.exchange/blog and https://www.amazon.com.au/Business-Development-Lawyers-Strategies-Getting/dp/1588521362

[137] An exception to this is where a few legal departments have tried to convert themselves from pure cost centres to profit centres. In most cases this will not be appropriate, but I mention it only as one specific example of business development.

[138] This point goes to the very heart of innovation that I will elaborate upon in the second book.

[139] In most cases this will be the entity that employs you in the case of an in-house lawyer and who engages your firm in the case of a law firm lawyer. However, if that entity is a subsidiary, then typically the parent company will strictly speaking be your client.

[140] We will explore this point further in chapter 8.

[141] *The Trusted Advisor.* David H. Maister, Charles H. Green, Robert M. Galford, Free Press; 20th Edition, February 2021

[142] https://www.acc.com/resource-library/if-other-hat-fits-wear-it-guide-effective-business-partnering

[143] This is an expression sometimes used to describe a situation where you are considered part of the business team on an informal if not a formal basis.
[144] Lawyers who do get into trouble do so because either they did not get involved in an illegal or unethical business decision, when they should have intervened, or turn a blind eye to the illegality or unethical aspects.
[145] The one situation where you may have some responsibility in relation to a business decision is where you have failed to comply with one of your professional duties as a lawyer as discussed elsewhere in the book.
[146] I explain this in more detail in the second book.
[147] This topic is discussed in more detail in chapter 8.
[148] https://corpgov.law.harvard.edu/2010/09/05/the-general-counsel-as-lawyer-statesman/
[149] Ibid endnote 14
[150] See for example *Improving Performance: How to Manage the White Space in the Organization Chart.* Geary A Rummler and Alan P Brache. Wiley, 3rd edition (November 2012)
[151] A detailed coverage of this point that I explore in my workshops is beyond the scope of this book. However, as an example, doing contract work is, contrary to the understanding of most lawyers, only expected of lawyers because lawyers decided the contracts were all necessary and that lawyers need to be involved. It does not always need to be so!
[152] Dan Heath, Avid Reader Press/Simon and Schuster, 3 March 2020
[153] See for example the UK Post Office case, the Star Casino case in Australia and Enron in the U.S
[154] The requirement to be independent can also sometimes be relevant to maintaining legal professional privilege in countries that have that concept.
[155] There are even suggestions that in-house lawyers need more regulatory protections and restrictions. See for example https://docs.google.com/document/d/e/2PACX-1vTsOgvh0qvOWK_kFXUUnqBct5bxHQuV3jzhDU9QwSbUUY59rJx4vjD1Pc5e9RSbZOt94emhyTrWNERS/pub
[156] The reason for that is because clients typically have a narrow view of what lawyers are capable of and therefore do not expect lawyers to be able to contribute much beyond legal advice and legal work.

[157] https://corpgov.law.harvard.edu/2016/03/29/the-inside-counsel-revolution/
[158] Also known as 'the practice of law'

[159] See for example,
https://www.olsc.nsw.gov.au/Documents/what_is_legal_work.pdf,
https://www.lawsociety.org.uk/public/for-public-visitors/resources/glossary#h3-heading12,
https://www.americanbar.org/groups/professional_responsibility/task_force_model_definition_practice_law/

[160] Steve Mark, the Legal Service Commissioner of NSW Australia was just referring to the situation in NSW, but his comment is broadly applicable .
https://www.olsc.nsw.gov.au/Documents/what_is_legal_work.pdf

[161] This also includes situations where, because of reimagining work, it no longer needs to be done by anybody in a legal department or firm. Generative AI, although by no means at the requisite standard yet for lawyers to not be involved in most legal work, has given everyone a very real indication of what technology can do. Such systems are only going to become increasingly capable over time.

[162] Ibid endnote 25

[163] Ibid endnote 26

[164] This has been the case historically. However, with the rapid automation of the type of work that junior lawyers typically start their careers doing, this may change somewhat and it may be that they start doing more internal business work and less legal work.

[165] See for example Rajah Tann Asia, featured in the second book, who had used the T-Shaped Lawyer Framework as the basis for their training and professional development of their one thousand legal professionals working in ten countries throughout Asia.

Made in the USA
Las Vegas, NV
16 March 2026

43726633R10125